CATCHIN' 'EM AIN'T NUTHIN'. IT'S GITTIN' 'EM HOME THAT'S HARD WORK.

"Any time a man ain't fishin' he's just fritterin' away his life."
—PATRICK F. MCMANUS, "I FISH; THEREFORE, I AM"

# 100 YEARS OF FISHING

## THE ULTIMATE TRIBUTE
## TO OUR FISHING TRADITION

From the Editors of Voyageur Press

With stories, artwork, and photographs from
Patrick F. McManus, P. J. O'Rourke, Norman Maclean,
Joan Salvato Wulff, Zane Grey, Ernest Hemingway,
Sigurd F. Olson, Gordon MacQuarrie, Robert Ruark,
Red Smith, Jimmy Carter, Nick Lyons,
Ron Schara, and more.

Voyageur Press

Edited by Amy Rost-Holtz and Michael Dregni
Book designed by Andrea Rud
Jacket designed by Kristy Tucker
Printed in Hong Kong

99    00    01    02    03    5    4    3    2    1

Library of Congress Cataloging-in-Publication Data
100 years of fishing : the ultimate tribute to our fishing tradition / from the editors of Voyageur Press ; with stories,
    artwork, and photographs from Patrick F. McManus . . . [et al.].
        p.    cm.
    ISBN 0-89658-430-5
    1. Fishing—United States Literary collections.  2. Fishing stories, American.  I. McManus, Patrick F.
II. Voyageur Press.  III. Title: One hundred years of fishing.
SH441.A14  1999
799.1'0973—dc21                    99-27420
                            CIP

Distributed in Canada by Raincoast Books, 8680 Cambie Street, Vancouver, B.C. V6P 6M9

Published by Voyageur Press, Inc.
123 North Second Street, P.O. Box 338, Stillwater, MN 55082 U.S.A.
651-430-2210, fax 651-430-2211

*Educators, fundraisers, premium and gift buyers, publicists, and marketing managers:* Looking for creative products and new sales ideas? Voyageur Press books are available at special discounts when purchased in quantities, and special editions can be created to your specifications. For details contact the marketing department at 800-888-9653.

ON THE FRONTISPIECE, CLOCKWISE FROM TOP LEFT: *Currier & Ives lithograph of a hooked trout, circa 1880; A day down at the old fishing hole from a 1950s Massey-Harris tractor brochure; Two proud anglers congratulate each other on their catch (Photograph courtesy of the Minnesota Historical Society); 1930s "tall-tale" postcard.*

PAGES 2–3, MAIN PHOTO: *A solitary angler casts for fish through the morning mist. (Photograph © Ron Spomer)*

PAGE 3, INSET: *"Ten of a Kind": A fine day's catch pictured on a 1940s postcard.*

# ACKNOWLEDGMENTS

Our thanks go to Dale Arenz; Tom Benda of Apple Creek Publishing; Lynette Dodson; Roper Green at the Green Agency for going out of his way to find additional information about fly rod making; Wayne Gudmundson; Howard Lambert; P. J. O'Rourke; Sarah Arnott Ozment; David E. Petzal, Executive Editor at *Field & Stream*; Ron Schara; Millard Wells; Roger Welsch for his "tall tale" postcards; and Bob White.

# CONTENTS

*A fly fisherman casts into a Montana stream after a spring snowfall. (Photograph © Alan and Sandy Carey)*

# INTRODUCTION

# "GONE FISHING"

"Gone fishing." Those two words evoke countless memories. Days spent wetting a line off the sun-baked dock of a cabin during a childhood summer long ago. Mornings on a favorite mountain trout stream, feeling the chill of the water through our waders as we cast the line through the mist to drop the fly into the calm of an eddy. Afternoons when work was slow and we packed up to go troll the big lake, hanging a note on the office door to let people know we wouldn't be back until tomorrow: "Gone fishing."

MAIN PHOTO: *With the mountains of Montana as a backdrop, a fly fisherman plays his trout. (Photograph © Bill Buckley/The Green Agency)*

INSET: *"Gone fishing": On a hot summer day, two youths stroll to the old fishing hole with their poles and cans of worms on this 1950s postcard.*

In these days of dizzying "progress" run rampant in an uncertain world, those two words—"gone fishing"—can be a source of great comfort. This century has borne witness to revolutionary changes in our culture, technology, and the natural world—many of which have been good, others that we may forever mourn. Faced with such important concerns, it's nice to know you can always step away from the hustle of the world and simply go fishing.

Few other endeavors invite such solace and contemplation. Like stepping into the silence of a grand cathedral or focusing in Zen meditation, fishing can refresh the body and renew the soul. Thus, it's little wonder that going fishing has become almost a philosophy of life for many. Bumper stickers proclaim that a bad day of fishing is better than a good day at the office, or that the driver would rather be fishing than doing just about anything else. For some, those are words to live by.

## A BRIEF HISTORY OF FISHING

Humans have taken food from the waters for millenia. In the beginning, people probably discovered that the lakes, rivers, and seas were plentiful with food in the form of fish, shellfish, and amphibious animals. According to archaeologists, the first means of catching these animals, around thirty thousand to forty thousand years ago, were spears, nets, traps, and hooks on animal-sinew lines. The concept of fishing was born.

The first images of anglers appeared in hieroglyphics drawn by the Egyptians some seven thousand years ago. One Egyptian painting from about four thousand years ago depicts people using nets to catch schools of fish, as well as a tool that looks to be a precursor of the fishing rod and line.

About 300 B.C., the Greek Theocritus penned the first description of fishing, writing of a "bait deceitfully dangling from the rod." The Chinese created silken fishing line and metal hooks that replaced the wood or bone hooks that were believed to be used up until about 200 B.C.

It has been over the past five centuries that fishing has become established as a sport. The first guidebook to the art of angling was written by a nun, Dame Juliana Barners, and was published in England in 1496 under the quaint title *The Treatise of Fyshynge Wyth an Angle*. In 1653, Izaak Walton's *The Compleat Angler* arrived, becoming the most famous book on the subject over the centuries with hundreds of editions published.

Today, interest in fishing is believed to be at an all-time zenith. Every weekend, thousands gather their tackle, dig worms from the backyard, or tie specially crafted flies, and head for the old fishing hole. Fishing is a North American institution—and big business. Some 60 million North Americans fish, more than the 24 million who play golf and the 17 million who play tennis combined; approximately one in every five North Americans hang out the "gone fishing" sign every year.

Bass is the fish most frequently sought, and North America's 30 million bass anglers alone are the basis of a $46 billion industry. According to United States Fish and Wildlife Service statistics, 43 percent of freshwater anglers fish for bass, 34 percent for panfish, 30 percent for catfish and bullhead, 30 percent for trout, and 28 percent for crappie.

At the same time, however, fish—and indeed all of the natural world—are threatened as never before. Factories, garbage dumps, and landfills pollute our water and kill fish. Farmlands and urban sprawl encroach on waterways. Boats and other recreational vehicles churn up valuable habitat. Over the next century, it will be up to all of us to work to preserve the natural world, our sport, and, in the end, ourselves.

## ABOUT *100 YEARS OF FISHING*

The writers gathered in this anthology include two presidents of the United States, one Pulitzer Prize winner, a Nobel Prize winner, several of the most popular novelists of the twentieth century, and a variety of outdoors writers made famous in the pages of *Field & Stream*, *Sports Afield*, and *Outdoor Life*. In addition, there are some ordinary Joes (and Janes) who simply love to fish and have a good yarn to tell.

This anthology is organized chronologically, providing an outline of our century's fishing history in literature. In addition, the writing itself gives a fascinating window into the changing styles of the different eras, from the flowery philosophical musings of the turn-of-the-century anglers to the hard-edged, high-adventure writing of the middle decades to a return to philosophy—as well as a healthy dose of humor—in current years.

Former U.S. President Grover Cleveland's sketch is typical of the 1900s, with its ornate prose celebrating

*The love of fishing often begins at an early age with nothing more than a can of worms dug up from the backyard, a penny hook, bamboo rod, a single sinker, and a handful of wooden bobbers. Memorabilia owners: Pete Press and Guy Chambers. (Photograph © Howard Lambert)*

the noble gentleman's sport of angling. Zane Grey, the master of the Western, wrote in a tough, no-holds-barred style packed with adventure, a style that Ernest Hemingway perfected in his own novels and short stories. Sigurd F. Olson wrote lyrically about the great outdoors, while Gordon MacQuarrie laughed at the trials and tribulations of anglers attempting to conquer that same wilderness.

Robert Ruark and Red Smith spoke of the relationship between grandfathers and younger generations and the lessons that were shared while fishing. Norman Maclean understood the relationship between religion and fly fishing and wrote about angling with a beauty and grace that may never be matched.

And then there are the humorous sketches of Patrick F. McManus and P. J. O'Rourke that poke fun at our favorite sport—and ourselves.

This is not just an anthology of writing, however. This book is also chock full of photographs from some of the best contemporary outdoors photographers, as well as historical images of anglers that speak across the years of times gone by. In addition, there are vintage advertisements, brochures, and artwork that tell of fishing trips when catching your limit was not just a dream.

If you can't pack your rod and reel to go fishing right now, you can at least curl up in front of the fireplace and turn through the pages of this book, reliving good times and great fishing trips.

ABOVE: *A six-year-old angler proudly displays her catch: an armful of rainbow trout caught on a fly rod. (Photograph © Ron Spomer)*

RIGHT: *A young angler wets his line in the waters of Oregon's Wallowa Lake as the rising sun's rays light the mountains above. (Photograph © Dennis Frates)*

# 100 YEARS OF FISHING

The real history of fishing dates back to the day when, as a child, each of us first hooked a worm and set out in dogged pursuit of the finny critters. Perhaps a grandparent taught you to fish for sunnies from a time-tested wooden rowboat. Perhaps it was a parent who showed you how to first cast a flyrod or an older sibling who steadied your arms as you reeled in a smallmouth bass.

The stories collected here are a record of that personal history of fishing over the past one hundred years. The end of a century and the dawn of a new one inspires us to pause and reflect on the changes in our lives; this book may serve as mnemonic, reviving memories of days past, fine fishing trips, old friends, and great catches.

MAIN PHOTO: *A fishing boat casts its shadow on Minnesota's Mantrap Lake during an early morning outing. (Photograph © Richard Hamilton Smith)*

INSET: *"Catch and Release—Rainbow Trout": a watercolor painting by Minnesota artist Bob White.*

# THE MISSION OF
# FISHING AND FISHERMEN

By Grover Cleveland

Stephen Grover Cleveland (1837–1908) was both the twenty-second and the twenty-fourth president of the United States, serving as the U.S. head of state in non–consecutive terms from 1885 to 1889 and from 1893 to 1897.

Alongside his career as a statesman, Cleveland harbored a lifelong love of the great outdoors. He was both a hunter and an angler, and wrote about his sporting adventures in *Fishing and Shooting Sketches* (1906). This book may seem an odd partner on a bookshelf next to Cleveland's other titles, such as *Principles and Purposes of Our Form of Government* (1892), but it shows where at least a part of his heart lay.

This selection from Cleveland's sporting collection is chock full of the earnest, philosophical musings typical of the deep feelings turn-of-the-century hunters and anglers had for their crafts.

*Days gone by: Two gentlemen anglers reel in their catch from the rapids of Sulpher Creek running through Platt National Park, Sulpher, Oklahoma, in 1902. (Photograph courtesy of the Western History Collections, University of Oklahoma Libraries)*

IT WAS QUITE a long time ago that a compelling sense of duty led me to undertake the exoneration of a noble fraternity, of which I am an humble member, from certain narrow-minded, if not malicious, accusations. The title given to what was then written, "A Defense of Fishermen," was precisely descriptive of its purpose. It was not easy, however, to keep entirely within defensive limits; for the temptation was very strong and constant to abandon negation and palliation for the more pleasing task of commending to the admiration and affection of mankind in affirmative terms both fishing and fishermen. A determination to attempt this at another time, and thus supplement the matter then in hand, made resistance to this temptation successful; but the contemplated supplementation was then foreshadowed in the following terms:

"The defense of the fishing fraternity which has been here attempted is by no means so completely stated as it should be. Nor should the world be allowed to overlook the admirable affirmative qualifies which exist among genuine members of the brotherhood and the useful traits which the indulgence in the gentle art cultivates and fosters. A recital of these, with a description of the personal influence of these peculiarities found in the ranks of fishermen, and the influence of these peculiarities on success or failure, are necessary to a thorough vindication of those who worthily illustrate the virtues of our clan."

The execution of the design thus foreshadowed has until now been evaded on account of the importance and delicacy of the undertaking and a distrust of my ability to deal adequately with the subject. Though these misgivings have not been overcome, my perplexity, as I enter upon the work so long delayed, is somewhat relieved by the hope that true fishermen will be tolerant, whatever may be the measure of my success, and that all others concerned will be teachable and open-minded.

## LESSONS THE FISHERMAN LEARNS FROM NATURE

The plan I have laid out for the treatment of my topic leads me, first of all, to speak of the manner in which the fishing habit operates upon man's nature for its betterment; and afterward to deal with the qualities of heart and disposition necessary to the maintenance of good and regular standing in the fishing fraternity.

There is no man in the world capable of profitable thought who does not know that the real worth and genuineness of the human heart are measured by its readiness to submit to the influences of Nature, and to appreciate the goodness of the Supreme Power who has made and beautified Nature's abiding-place. In this domain, removed from the haunts of men and far away from the noise and dust of their turmoil and strife, the fishing that can fully delight the heart of the true fisherman is found; and here in its enjoyment, those who fish are led, consciously or unconsciously, to a quiet but distinct recognition of a power greater than man's, and a goodness far above human standards. Amid such surroundings and within such influences no true fisherman, whether sensitively attuned to sublime suggestion, or of a coarser mold and apparently intent only upon a successful catch, can fail to receive impressions which so elevate the soul and soften the heart as to make him a better man.

It is known of all men that one of the rudiments in the education of a true fisherman is the lesson of patience. If he has a natural tendency in this direction it must be cultivated. If such a tendency is lacking he must acquire patience by hard schooling. This quality is so indispensable in fishing circles that those who speak of a patient fisherman waste their words. In point of fact, and properly speaking, there can be no such thing as an impatient fisherman. It cannot, therefore, be denied that in so far as fishing is a teacher of the virtue of patience, it ought to be given a large item of credit in reckoning its relation to the everyday affairs of life; for certainly the potency of patience as a factor in all worldly achievements and progress cannot be overestimated. If faith can move mountains, patience and faith combined ought to move the universe.

Moreover, if those who fish must be patient, no one should fail to see that patience is a most desirable national trait and that it is vastly important to our body politic that there should continue among our people a large contingent of well-equipped fishermen, constantly prepared and willing to contribute to their country's fund of blessings a liberal and pure supply of this saving virtue.

To those who are satisfied with a superficial view of the subject it may seem impossible that the dili-

*These century-old baits and tackle are fine examples of the distinctive craftsmanship and design of the romantic Victorian times. The prize lure in this photograph, located in the handmade wood-and-leather tackle box's cover, is the American Spinner made by John B. McHarg. Among the other lures and fishing equipment shown in their original packaging is the Adirondack Spinner. Memorabilia owner: Northland Fishing Museum of Osseo, Wisconsin. (Photograph © Howard Lambert)*

gence and attention necessary to a fisherman's success can leave him any opportunity, while fishing, to thoughtfully contemplate any matter not related to his pursuit. Such a conception of the situation cannot be indorsed for a moment by those of us who are conversant with the mysterious and unaccountable mental phenomena which fishing develops. We know that the true fisherman finds no better time for profitable contemplation and mental exercise than when actually engaged with his angling outfit. It will probably never be possible for us to gather statistics showing the moving sermons, the enchanting poems, the learned arguments and eloquent orations that have been composed or constructed between the bites, strikes or rises of fish; but there can be no doubt that of the many intellectual triumphs won in every walk of life a larger proportion has been actually hooked and landed with a rod and reel by those of the fishing fraternity than have been secured in any one given condition of the non-fishing world.

This may appear to be a bold statement. It is intended as an assertion that fishing and fishermen have had much to do with the enlightenment and elevation of humanity. In support of this proposition volumes might be written; but only a brief array of near-at-hand evidence will be here presented.

Those who have been fortunate enough to hear the fervid eloquence of Henry Ward Beecher, and even those who have only read what he has written, cannot overlook his fishing propensity—so constantly manifest that the things he said and wrote were fairly redolent of fishing surroundings. His own specific confession of fealty was not needed to entitle him to the credentials of a true fisherman, nor to disclose one of the never-failing springs of his best inspiration. When these things are recalled, and when we contemplate the lofty mission so well performed by this noble angler, no member of our brotherhood can do better in its vindication than to point to his career as proof of what the fishing habit has done for humanity.

## WHAT MASHPEE WATERS DID FOR WEBSTER

Daniel Webster, too, was a fisherman—always in good and regular standing. In marshaling the proof which his great life furnishes of the beneficence of the fishing propensity, I approach the task with a feeling of awe quite natural to one who has slept in the room occupied by the great Expounder during his fishing campaigns on Cape Cod and along the shores of Mashpee Pond and its adjacent streams. This distinguished member of our fraternity was an industrious and attentive fisherman. He was, besides, a wonderful orator—and largely so because he was a fisherman. He himself has confessed to the aid he received from a fishing environment in the preparation of his best oratorical efforts; and other irrefutable testimony to the same effect is at hand.

It is not deemed necessary to cite in proof of such aid more than a single incident. Perhaps none of Mr. Webster's orations was more notable, or added more to his lasting fame, than that delivered at the laying of the cornerstone of the Bunker Hill Monument. And it will probably be conceded that its most impressive and beautiful passage was addressed to the survivors of the War of Independence then present, beginning with the words, "Venerable men!" This thrilling oratorical flight was composed and elaborated by Mr. Webster while wading waist deep and casting his flies in Mashpee waters. He himself afterward often referred to this circumstance; and one who was his companion on this particular occasion has recorded the fact that, noticing indications of laxity in fishing action on Mr. Webster's part, he approached him, and that, in the exact words of this witness, "he seemed to be gazing at the overhanging trees, and presently advancing one foot and extending his right hand he commenced to speak, 'Venerable Men!'"

## MR. WEBSTER'S REMARKS TO A FISH

Though this should be enough to support conclusively the contention that incidents of Mr. Webster's great achievements prove the close relationship between fishing and the loftiest attainments of mankind, this branch of our subject ought not to be dismissed without reference to a conversation I once had with old John Attaquin, then a patriarch among the few survivors of the Mashpee Indians. He had often been Mr. Webster's guide and companion on his fishing trips and remembered clearly many of their happenings. It was with a glow of love and admiration amounting almost to worship that he related how this great fisherman, after landing a large trout on the bank of the stream, "talked mighty strong and fine to that fish and told him what a mistake he had made, and what a fool he was to take that fly, and that he would have been all right if he had let it alone." Who can doubt that patient search would disclose, somewhere in Mr. Webster's speeches and writings, the elaboration, with high intent, of that "mighty strong and fine" talk addressed to the fish at Mashpee?

The impressive story of this simple, truthful old Indian was delightfully continued when, with the enthusiasm of an untutored mind remembering pleasant sensations, the narrator told how the great fisherman and orator having concluded his "strong, fine talk," would frequently suit the action to the word, when he turned to his guide and proposed a fitting libation in recognition of his catch. This part of the story is not here repeated on account of its superior value as an addition to the evidence we have already gathered, but I am thus given an opportunity to speak of the emotion which fascinated me as the story proceeded, and as I recalled how precisely a certain souvenir called "the Webster Flask," carefully hoarded among my valued possessions, was fitted to the situation described.

Let it be distinctly understood that the claim is not here made that all who fish can become as great as

*Fishing at the turn of the century was a gentleman's pursuit, and a fly-fishing gentleman simply could not fish without a well-tied necktie and a waxed handlebar mustache. This painting by Sherman Foote Denton (1856–1937) evokes a bygone era of the sporting outdoors.*

Henry Ward Beecher or Daniel Webster. It is insisted, however, that fishing is a constructive force, capable of adding to and developing the best there is in any man who fishes in a proper spirit and among favorable surroundings. In other words, it is claimed that upon the evidence adduced it is impossible to avoid the conclusion that the fishing habit, by promoting close association with Nature, by teaching patience, and by generating or stimulating useful contemplation, tends directly to the increase of the intellectual power of its votaries, and, through them, to the improvement of our national character.

In pursuance of the plan adopted for the presentation of our subject, mention must now be made of the qualities of heart and disposition absolutely essential to the maintenance of honorable membership in the fishing fraternity. This mode of procedure is not only made necessary by the exigencies of our scheme, but the brotherhood of fishermen would not be satisfied if the exploitation of their service to humanity and their value to the country should terminate with a recital of the usefulness of their honorable pursuit. The record would be woefully incomplete if reference were omitted to the relation of fishing to the moral characteristics and qualities of heart, with which it is as vitally connected as with the intellectual traits already mentioned.

No man can be a completely good fisherman unless within his piscatorial sphere he is generous, sympathetic and honest. If he expects to enjoy that hearty and unrestrained confidence of his brethren in the fraternity which alone can make his membership a comfort and a delight, he must be generous to the point of willingness to share his last leaders and flies, or any other items of his outfit, with any worthy fellow-fisherman who may be in need. The manifestation of littleness and crowding selfishness often condoned in other quarters, and the over-reaching conduct so generally permitted in business circles, are unpardonable crimes in the true fisherman's code.

Of course, there is nothing to prevent those from fishing who wholly disregard all rules of generosity, fairness and decency. Nor can we of the brotherhood of true fishermen always shield ourselves from the re-proach to which we are subjected by those who steal our livery and disgrace it by casting aside all manly liberality in their intercourse with other fishermen and all considerate self-restraint in their intercourse with fish. We constantly deprecate the existence of those called by our name, in whose low conception of the subject, fishing is but a greedy game, where selfishness and meanness are the winning cards, and where the stakes are the indiscriminate and ruthless slaughter of fish; and let it be here said, once for all, that with these we have nothing to do except to condemn them as we pass. Our concern is with true fishermen—a very different type of mankind—and with those who *prima facie* have some claim to the title.

## How to Know a True Fisherman

No burdensome qualifications or tedious probation obstruct the entrance to this fraternity; but skill and fishing ability count for nothing in eligibility. The oldest and most experienced and skillful fisherman will look with composure upon the vanishing chances of his catch through the floundering efforts of an awkward beginner, if the awkward flounderer has shown that he is sound at heart. He may not fish well, but if he does not deliberately rush ahead of all companions to pre-empt every promising place in the stream, nor everlastingly study to secure for his use the best of the bait, nor always fail to return borrowed tackle, nor prove to be blind, deaf and dumb when others are in tackle need, nor crowd into another's place, nor draw his flask in secrecy, nor light a cigar with no suggestion of another, nor do a score of other indefinable mean things that among true fishermen constitute him an unbearable nuisance, he will not only be tolerated but aided in every possible way.

It is curious to observe how inevitably the brotherhood discovers unworthiness. Even without an overt act it is detected—apparently by a sort of instinct. In any event, and in spite of the most cunning precautions, the sin of the unfit is sure to find them out; and no excuse is allowed to avert unforgiving ostracism as its punishment.

A true fisherman is conservative, provident, not

*Staring out from its lair beneath a fallen tree, a largemouth bass takes aim on an L. L. Bean bass plug. (Photograph © Doug Stamm/ ProPhoto)*

*A trio of well-dressed women try their luck with bamboo poles on Oklahoma's Washita River circa 1900. Their armed male chaperone keeps watch. (Photograph courtesy of Western History Collections, University of Oklahoma Libraries)*

given to envy, considerate of the rights of others, and careful of his good name. He fishes many a day and returns at night to his home, hungry, tired and disappointed; but he still has faith in his methods, and is not tempted to try new and more deadly lures. On the contrary, he is willing in all circumstances to give the fish the chance for life which a liberal sporting disposition has determined to be their due; and he will bide his time under old conditions. He will not indulge his fishing propensity to the extent of the wanton destruction and waste of fish; he will not envy the superior advantages of another in the indulgence of the pastime he loves so well; he will never be known to poach upon the preserves of a fortunate neighbor; and no one will be quicker or more spirited than he in the defense of his fishing honor and character.

## TRUTH AS DEFINED BY THE HONORABLE GUILD

This detailed recital of the necessary qualifications of good fishermanship serves most importantly as the prelude of an invitation for skeptics to observe the complete identity of these qualifications with the factors necessary to good citizenship, and from thence to concede a more ready recognition of the honorable place which should be awarded to the fraternity among the agencies of our country's good.

In conclusion, and to the end that there should be no appearance of timidity or lack of frankness, something should be said explanatory of the degree and kind of truthfulness which an honorable standing in the fishing fraternity exacts. Of course, the notion must not be for a moment tolerated that deliberate, downright lying as to an essential matter is permissible. It must be confessed, however, that unescapable traditions and certain inexorable conditions of our brotherhood tend to a modification of the standards of truthfulness which have been set up in other quarters. Beyond doubt, our members should be as reliable in statement as our traditions and full enjoyment of fraternity membership will permit.

An attempt has been made to remedy the indefiniteness of this requirement by insisting that no statement should be regarded as sufficiently truthful for the fisherman's code that had not for its foundation at least

*For a small fish, a bluegill can put up a ferocious fight. (Photograph © Doug Stamm/ProPhoto)*

a belief of its correctness on the part of the member making it. This was regarded as too much elasticity in the quality of the belief required. The matter seems to have been finally adjusted in a manner expressed in the motto:"In essentials—truthfulness; in non-essentials—reciprocal latitude." If it is objected that there may be great difficulty and perplexity in determining what are essentials and what non-essentials under this rule, it should be remembered that no human arrangements, especially those involving morals and ethics, can be made to fit all emergencies.

In any event, great comfort is to be found in the absolute certainty that the law of truthfulness will be so administered by the brotherhood that no one will ever be permitted to suffer in mind, body or estate by reason of fishermen's tales.

# BIG TUNA

## By Zane Grey

Pearl Zane Grey (1872–1939) was a dentist in New York City with aspirations of being a writer. In 1907, he traveled to the American West, a trip that would change his life. With visions of the Wild West dancing in his head, he embarked on a career writing short stories for the "pulp" magazines and dimestore novels that were then coming into their heyday. His novels, such as *Riders of the Purple Sage* (1912), helped create the genre of the Great American Western—and in turn, made him one of the most popular American writers of all time.

Grey was also an avid hunter and fisherman, and was prolific in penning accounts of outdoors treks for fledgling magazines such as *Field & Stream* and *Outdoor Life*.

This piece first appeared in *Field & Stream* in 1919 and was typical of Grey's writing, packed with high adventure and true-life daring.

*A litter of curious kittens circles the tail of a tarpon hung out on the docks of Key West, Florida, in this watercolor painting by Millard Wells. Blending his hobbies of saltwater fly fishing and painting, Wells has fished and painted much of the Florida Keys and the region, from Grand Cayman to the Yucatan Peninsula. His work has been shown at museums and galleries from the National Gallery of Art in Washington, D.C. to his own Wells Studio-Gallery in Islamorada, Florida.*

IT TOOK ME five seasons at Catalina to catch a big tuna. And the event was so thrilling that I had to write to my fishermen friends about it. The results of my effusions seem rather dubious. Robert H. Davis, editor of *Munsey's,* replies in this wise: "If you went out with a mosquito net to catch a mess of minnows, your story would read like Roman gladiators seining the Tigris for whales."

Now I am at a loss to know how to take that compliment. Davis goes on to say more, and he also quotes me: "You say 'the hard diving fight of a tuna liberates the brute instinct in a man.'—Well, Zane, it also liberates the qualities of a liar!"

Davis does not love the sweet, soft scent that breathes from off the sea. Once on the Jersey coast I went tuna fishing with him. He was not happy on the boat. But once he came up out of the cabin with a jaunty feather in his hat. I admired it. I said: "Bob, I'll have to get something like that for my hat."

"Zane," he replied, piercingly, "what you need for your hat is a head!"

My lucky day came after no tuna had been reported for a week. Captain Dan and I ran out off Silver Canyon just on a last forlorn hope. The sea was rippling white and blue, with a good breeze. No whales showed. We left Avalon about one o'clock, ran out five miles, and began to fish. Our methods had undergone some change. We used a big kite out on three hundred yards of line; we tied this line on my leader; and we tightened the drag on the reel so that it took a nine pound pull to start the line off. This seemed a fatal procedure, but I was willing to try anything. My hope of getting a strike was exceedingly slim. Instead of a flying-fish for bait we used a good sized smelt, and we used hooks, big and strong, and sharp as needles.

We had not been out half an hour when Captain Dan left the wheel and jumped up on the gunwale to look at something.

"What do you see?" I asked, eagerly.

He was silent a moment. I daresay he did not want to make any mistakes. Then he jumped back to the wheel.

"School of tuna!" he boomed.

I stood up and looked in the direction indicated, but I could not see them. Dan said only the movement on the water could be seen. Good long swells were running, rather high, and presently I did see tuna showing darkly bronze in the blue water. They vanished. We had to turn the boat somewhat, and it began to appear that we would have difficulty in putting the bait into the school. So it turned out. We were in the wrong quarter to use the wind. I saw the school of tuna go by, perhaps two hundred feet from the boat. They were traveling fast, somewhat under the surface, and were separated from each other. They were big tuna. Captain Dan said they were hungry hunting fish. To me they appeared game, swift and illusive.

We lost sight of them. With the boat turned fairly into the west wind the kite soared, pulling hard, and my bait skipped down the slopes of the swells and up over the crests just like a live leaping little fish. It was my opinion that the tuna were running inshore. Dan said they were headed west. We saw nothing of them. Again the old familiar disappointment knocked at my heart, with added bitterness of past defeat. Dan scanned the sea like a shipwrecked mariner watching for a sail.

"I see them! . . . There!" he called. "They're sure traveling fast."

That stimulated me with a shock. I looked and looked, but I could not see the darkened water. Moments passed, during which I stood up, watching my bait as it slipped over the waves. I knew Dan would tell me when to begin to jump it. The suspense grew to be intense.

"We'll catch up with them," said Dan, excitedly. "Everything's right now. Kite high, pulling hard—bait working fine. You're sure of a strike. . . . When you see one set the bait hook quick and hard."

The ambition of years, the long patience, the endless efforts, the numberless disappointments, flashed up at Captain Dan's words of certainty, and, together with the thrilling proximity of the tuna we were chasing, they roused in me emotion utterly beyond proportion or reason. This had happened to me before, notably in swordfishing, but never had I felt such thrills, such tingling nerves, such oppression on my chest, such a wild eager rapture. It would have been impossible, notwithstanding my emotional temperament, if the leading up to this moment had not included so much long-sustained feeling.

"Jump your bait! " called Dan, with a ring in his

*A hooked sailfish makes a run in this painting by renowned wildlife artist Lynn Bogue Hunt. A prolific artist, Hunt's works graced the covers of most of the major North American outdoors magazines as well as catalogs from sporting goods manufacturers such as Remington and others.*

*This saltwater fly fisherman has hooked a fierce barracuda, who won't give up without a fight. (Photograph © Doug Stamm / ProPhoto)*

*A fly fisherman makes one last cast from his anchored boat as the sun goes down on another day of Florida saltwater fishing. (Photograph © Bill Buckley/The Green Agency)*

ABOVE: *A tarpon makes a powerful leap in an attempt to spit out the lure in this watercolor by Florida Keys artist Millard Wells.*

FACING PAGE: *A pair of boats head into port after the last catch of the day. (Photograph © Henry F. Zeman)*

voice. "In two jumps you'll be in the tail-enders."

I jerked my rod. The bait gracefully leaped over a swell—shot along the surface, and ended with a splash. Again I jerked. As the bait rose into the air a huge angry splash burst just under it, and a broad-backed tuna lunged and turned clear over, his tail smacking the water.

"Jump it!" yelled Dan.

Before I could move a circling smash of white surrounded my bait. I heard it. With all my might I jerked. Strong and heavy came the weight of the tuna. I had hooked him. With one solid thumping splash he sounded. Here was test for line and test for me. I could not resist one turn of the thumb-wheel, to ease the drag. He went down with the same old incomparable speed. I saw the kite descending. Dan threw out the clutch—ran to my side. The reel screamed. Every tense

second, as the line whizzed off, I expected it to break. There was no joy, no sport in that painful watching. He ran off two hundred feet—then marvelous to see—he slowed up. The kite was still high, pulling hard. What with kite and drag and friction of line in the water that tuna had great strain upon him. He ran off a little more, slower this time, then stopped. The kite began to flutter.

I fell into the chair, jammed the rod-butt into the socket, and began to pump and wind.

"Doc, you're hooked on and you've stopped him!" boomed Dan. His face beamed. "Look at your legs!"

It became manifest then that my knees were wobbling, my feet puttering around, my whole lower limbs shaking as if I had the palsy. I had lost control of my lower muscles. It was funny; it was ridiculous. It showed just what was my state of excitement.

The kite fluttered down to the water. The kite-line had not broken off, and this must add severely to the strain on the fish. Not only had I stopped the tuna but soon I had him coming up, slowly, yet rather easily. He was directly under the boat. When I had all save about one hundred feet of line wound in the tuna anchored himself and would not budge for fifteen minutes. Then again rather easily he was raised fifty more feet. He acted like any small hard-fighting fish.

"I've hooked a little one," I began. "That big fellow—he missed the bait, and a small one grabbed it."

Dan would not say so, but he feared just that. What miserable black luck! Almost I threw the rod and reel overboard. Some sense, however, prevented me from such an absurdity. And as I worked the tuna closer and closer I grew absolutely sick with disappointment. The only thing to do was to haul this little fish in and go hunt up the school. So I pumped and pulled. That half hour seemed endless and bad business altogether. Anger possessed me and I began to work harder. At this juncture Shorty's boat appeared close to us. Shorty and Adams waved congratulations, and then made motions to Dan to get the direction of the school of tuna. That night both Shorty and Adams told me that I was working very hard on the fish, too hard to save any strength for a long battle.

Captain Dan watched the slow steady bends of my rod, as the tuna plugged, and at last he said: "Doc, it's a big fish!"

Strange to relate this did not electrify me. I did not believe it. But at the end of that half hour the tuna came clear to the surface, about one hundred feet from us, and there he rode the swells. Doubt folded his sable wings! Bronze and blue and green and silver flashes illumined the swells. I plainly saw that not only was the tuna big, but he was one of the long, slim, hard-fighting species.

Presently he sounded, and I began to work. I was fresh, eager, strong, and I meant to whip him quickly. Working on a big tuna is no joke. It is a man's job. A tuna fights on his side with head down and he never stops. If the angler rests the tuna will not only rest, too, but he will take more and more line. The method is a long slow lift or pump of rod—then lower the rod quickly and wind the reel. When the tuna is raised so high he will refuse to come any higher, and then there

is a deadlock. There lives no fisherman but what there lives a tuna that can take the conceit and the fight out of him.

For an hour I worked. I sweat and panted and burned in the hot sun; and I enjoyed it. The sea was beautiful. A strong salty fragrance, wet and sweet, floated on the breeze. Catalina showed clear and bright, with its colored cliffs and yellow slides and dark ravines. Clemente Island rose a dark long barren lonely land to the southeast. The clouds in the west were like trade-wind clouds, white, regular, with level base-line.

At the end of the second hour I was tiring. There came a subtle change of spirit and mood. I had never let up for a minute. Captain Dan praised me, vowed I had never fought either broadbill or roundbill swordfish so consistently hard, but he cautioned me to save myself.

"That's a big tuna," he said, as he watched my rod.

Most of the time we drifted. Some of the time Dan ran the boat to keep even with the tuna, so he could not get too far under the stern and cut the line. At intervals the fish appeared to let up and at others he plugged harder. This I discovered was merely that he fought the hardest when I worked the hardest. Once we gained enough on him to cut the tangle of kite-line that had caught some fifty feet above my leader. This afforded cause for less anxiety.

"I'm afraid of sharks," said Dan.

Sharks are the bane of tuna fishermen. More tuna are cut off by sharks than are ever landed by anglers. This made me redouble my efforts, and in half an hour more I was dripping wet, burning hot, aching all over, and so spent I had to rest. Every time I dropped the rod on the gunwale the tuna took line—zee—zee—zee— foot by foot and yard by yard. My hands were cramped; my thumbs red and swollen, almost raw. I asked Dan for the harness, but he was loath to put it on because he was afraid I would break the fish off. So I worked on and on, with spurts of fury and periods of lagging.

At the end of three hours I was in bad condition. I had saved a little strength for the finish, but I was in danger of using that up before the crucial moment arrived. Dan had put the harness on me. I knew afterward that it saved the day. By the aid of the harness, putting my shoulders into the lift, I got the double line over the reel, only to lose it. Every time the tuna was pulled near the boat he sheered off, and it did not appear possible for me to prevent it. He got into a habit of coming to the surface about thirty feet out, and hanging there, in plain sight, as if he was cabled to the rocks of the ocean. Watching him only augmented my trouble. It had ceased long ago to be fun or sport or game. It was now a fight and it began to be torture. My hands were all blisters—my thumbs raw. The respect I had for that tuna was great.

He plugged down mostly, but latterly he began to run off to each side, to come to the surface, showing his broad green-silver side, and then he weaved to and fro behind the boat, trying to get under it. Captain Dan would have to run ahead to keep away from him. To hold what gain I had on the tuna was at these periods almost unendurable. Where before I had sweat, burned, throbbed and ached, I now began to see red, to grow dizzy, to suffer cramps and nausea, and exceeding pain.

Three hours and a half showed the tuna slower, heavier, higher, easier. He had taken us fifteen miles from where we had hooked him. He was weakening, but I thought I was worse off then he was. Dan changed the harness. It seemed to make more effort possible.

The floor under my feet was wet and slippery from the salt water dripping off my reel. I could not get any footing. The bend of that rod downward, the ceaseless tug, tug, the fear of sharks, the paradoxical loss of desire now to land the tuna, the change in my feeling of ela-

tion and thrill to wonder, disgust and utter weariness of spirit and body,—all these warned me that I was at the end of my tether, and if anything could be done it must be.

Relaxing I took a short rest. Then nerving myself to be indifferent to the pain, and yielding altogether to the brutal instinct this tuna fighting rouses in a fisherman, I lay back with might and main. Eight times I had gotten the double line over the reel. On the ninth I shut down, clamped with my thumbs and froze there. The wire leader sang like a telephone wire in the cold. I could scarcely see. My arms cracked. I felt an immense strain that must break me in an instant.

Captain Dan reached the leader. Slowly he heaved. The strain upon me was released. I let go the reel, threw off the drag, and stood up. There the tuna was, the bronze and blue-backed devil, gaping, wide-eyed, shining and silvery as he rolled, a big tuna if there ever was one, and he was conquered.

When Dan lunged with the gaff the tuna made a tremendous splash that deluged us. Then Dan yelled for another gaff. I was quick to get it. Next it was for me to throw a lasso over that threshing tail. When I accomplished this the tuna was ours. We hauled him up on the stern, heaving, thumping, throwing water and blood, and even vanquished he was magnificent. Three hours and fifty minutes! As I fell back in a chair, all in, I could not see for my life why any fisherman would want to catch more than one large tuna.

# THE BEST RAINBOW
# TROUT FISHING

## By Ernest Hemingway

Ernest Miller Hemingway (1899–1961) needs little introduction. The author of *The Sun Also Rises* (1926), *A Farewell to Arms* (1929), *For Whom the Bell Tolls* (1940), and numerous other novels, short stories, and essays, Hemingway won the Nobel Prize for literature in 1954 following publication of his tour-de-force novella, *The Old Man and the Sea* (1952).

He got his start as a cub reporter for the Kansas City *Star* before moving on to the Toronto *Star*. This journalistic writing experience shaped his style of spare prose, terse declarative statements, and dialogue that almost lived and breathed.

This newspaper article appeared in the Toronto *Star Weekly* on August 28, 1920, and shows two of Hemingway's passions in embryo: his signature writing style and his love for fishing.

*"Fly fishing takes you to spectacular places and gives you a reason for being there that is far more compelling than just looking at the scenery. You become a participant, rather than a spectator; the creatures of the watery world become an extension of those things you care about, almost like family and friends." —Joan Salvato Wulff, *Joan Wulff's Fly Fishing* (Photograph © Richard Hamilton Smith)*

Rainbow trout fishing is as different from brook fishing as prize fighting is from boxing. The rainbow is called *Salmo iridescens* by those mysterious people who name the fish we catch and has recently been introduced into Canadian waters. At present the best rainbow trout fishing in the world is in the rapids of the Canadian Soo.

There the rainbow have been taken as large as fourteen pounds from canoes that are guided through the rapids and halted at the pools by OjIbway and Chippewa boatmen. It is a wild and nerve-frazzling sport and the odds are in favor of the big trout who tear off thirty or forty yards of line at a rush and then will sulk at the base of a big rock and refuse to be stirred into action by the pumping of a stout fly rod aided by a fluent monologue of Ojibwayian profanity. Sometimes it takes two hours to land a really big rainbow under those circumstances.

The Soo affords great fishing. But it is a wild nightmare kind of fishing that is second only in strenuousness to angling for tuna off Catalina Island. Most of the trout too take a spinner and refuse a fly and to the 99 per cent pure fly fisherman, there are no one hundred per centers, that is a big drawback.

Of course the rainbow trout of the Soo will take a fly but it is rough handling them in that tremendous volume of water on the light tackle a fly fisherman loves. It is dangerous wading in the spots that can be waded, too, for a misstep will take the angler over his head in the rapids. A canoe is a necessity to fish the very best water.

Altogether it is a rough, tough, mauling game, lacking in the meditative qualities of the Izaak Walton school of angling. What would make a fitting Valhalla for the good fisherman when he dies would be a regular trout river with plenty of rainbow trout in it jumping crazy for the fly.

There is such a one not forty miles from the Soo called the—well, called the river. It is about as wide as a river should be and a little deeper than a river ought to be and to get the proper picture you want to imagine in rapid succession the following fade-ins:

A high pine covered bluff that rises steep up out of the shadows. A short sand slope down to the river and a quick elbow turn with a little flood wood jammed in the bend and then a pool.

A pool where the moselle colored water sweeps into a dark swirl and expanse that is blue-brown with depth and fifty feet across.

There is the setting.

The action is supplied by two figures that slog into the picture up the trail along the river bank with loads on their backs that would tire a pack horse. These loads are pitched over the heads onto the patch of ferns by the edge of the deep pool. That is incorrect. Really the figures lurch a little forward and the lump line loosens and the pack slumps onto the ground. Men don't pitch loads at the end of an eight mile hike.

One of the figures looks up and notes the bluff is flattened on top and that there is a good place to put a tent. The other is lying on his back and looking straight up in the air. The first reaches over and picks up a grasshopper that is stiff with the fall of the evening dew and tosses him into the pool.

The hopper floats spraddle legged on the water of the pool an instant, an eddy catches him and then there is a yard long flash of flame, and a trout as long as your forearm has shot into the air and the hopper has disappeared.

"Did you see that?" gasped the man who had tossed in the grasshopper.

It was a useless question, for the other, who a moment before would have served as a model for a study entitled "Utter Fatigue," was jerking his fly rod out of the case and holding a leader in his mouth.

We decided on a McGinty and a Royal Coachman for the flies and at the second cast there was a swirl like the explosion of a depth bomb, the line went taut and the rainbow shot two feet out of water. He tore down the pool and the line went out until the core of the reel showed. He jumped and each time he shot into the air we lowered the tip and prayed. Finally he jumped and the line went slack and Jacques reeled in. We thought he was gone and then he jumped right under our faces. He had shot upstream towards us so fast that it looked as though he were off.

When I finally netted him and rushed him up the bank and could feel his huge strength in the tremendous muscular jerks he made when I held him flat against the bank, it was almost dark. He measured twenty-six inches and weighed nine pounds and seven ounces.

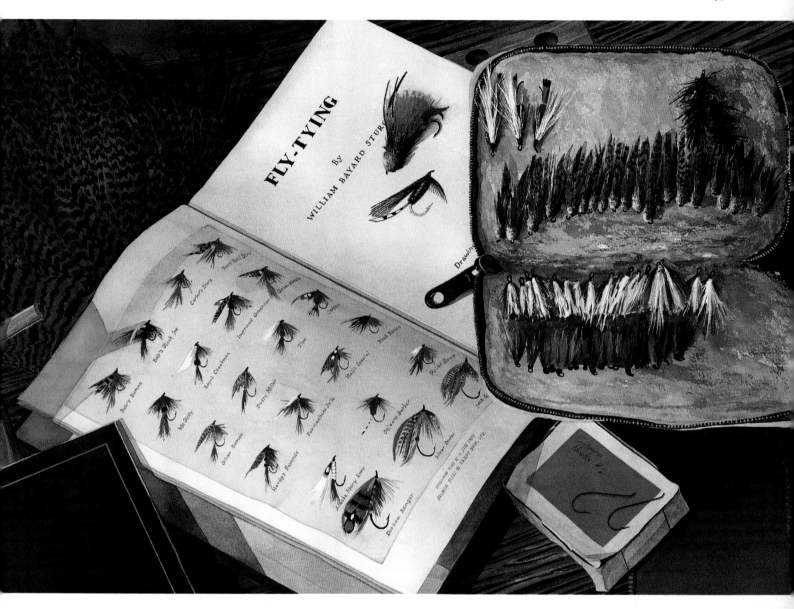

*"Somethings Old, Somethings New—Fly Tying Materials"* is a watercolor painted by Minnesota artist Bob White. Along with his painting, White works as an outdoors photographer and a professional fishing guide, leading treks as far afield as Alaska and Argentina. His Whitefish Studio is located in Marine-on-St.-Croix, Minnesota.

That is rainbow trout fishing.

The rainbow takes the fly more willingly than he does bait. The McGinty, a fly that looks like a yellow jacket, is the best. It should be tied on a number eight or ten hook.

The smaller flies get more strikes but are too small to hold the really big fish. The rainbow trout will live in the same streams with brook trout but they are found in different kinds of places. Brook trout will be forced into the shady holes under the bank and where alders hang over the banks, and the rainbow will dominate the clear pools and the fast shallows.

Magazine writers and magazine covers to the contrary the brook or speckled trout does not leap out of water after he has been hooked. Given plenty of line he will fight a deep rushing fight. Of course if you hold the fish too tight he will be forced by the rush of the current to flop on top of the water.

But the rainbow always leaps on a slack or tight line. His leaps are not mere flops, either, but actual jumps out of and parallel with the water of from a foot to five feet. A five-foot jump by any fish sounds improbable, but it is true.

If you don't believe it tie onto one in fast water and try and force him. Maybe if he is a five-pounder he will throw me down and only jump four feet eleven inches.

*Classic fly-fishing gear from the good old days. (Photograph © Jack Bissell)*

FACING PAGE: *A well-fought catch: a healthy-sized rainbow trout rests alongside a net and rod and reel. (Photograph © Doug Stamm/ProPhoto)*

*As the morning sun lights the treetops, a fly fisherman casts into a Montana stream. (Photograph © Alan and Sandy Carey)*

# FISHING JEWELRY

## By Sigurd F. Olson

Sigurd Olson (1899–1982) was a modern-day voyageur, born centuries after the first voyageurs paddled the waters of northern Minnesota. His numerous books of wilderness writings marked him as a transcendentalist in the fashion of Henry David Thoreau, sharing through his writing his conviction that the solitude of nature was a basic need of all human beings.

Olson's first book, *The Singing Wilderness* (1956), sang the praises of nature. It was followed by numerous other books and collections of essays and articles, including *Listening Point* (1958), *The Lonely Land* (1961), *Runes of the North* (1963), and *Open Horizons* (1969). Olson's writing—and his life—was devoted to understanding, explaining, and protecting the wilderness for future generations.

This article was first published in the Milwaukee *Journal* in 1925 and offers Olson's take on a theme often voiced in essays on angling: the debate between good, old-fashioned live bait versus the new-fangled lures, which Olson jokingly denounces as "fishing jewelry."

*"Fishing jewelry": a treasure trove of vintage fishing equipment in a well-used tackle box. (Photograph © Jack Bissell)*

THE TWO OF US, "Wild Cat" Dan and I had just stowed away enough fish mulligan to last us a week and were enduring the ominous silence that always comes between such an achievement and the inevitable suggestion, "Well guess we'd better clean up the mess."

After some fifteen minutes of bliss, I looked at Dan and he at me, both with the same blank expression of helplessness. Finally Dan heaved a ponderous sigh and rose to his feet. "Well," he started in, "I suppose," and he looked at me rather pleadingly, "I guess partner, I've et too much. Let's leave the dishes tills mornin'."

"Good idea Dan," answered I, greatly relieved. "Guess we both feel the same way."

With one accord, we pushed the supper dishes to the end of the table, just far enough back in the dark, so that they couldn't reproach us visibly at least for not washing them. It was all we could do after that, to stagger over to our respective bunks. Our pipes were soon going and a feeling of lazy comfort and peace pervaded the cabin.

As I watched the blue smoke curl up around the rafters, I wouldn't have traded places then with anyone else in the world. I knew then as I have often known since, that there is nothing so soul-satisfying and conducive to perfect contentment, as a full stomach and a good place to rest, after a day in the brush. Then to top it off, the rain began to patter softly against the south windows. The hour was ripe for dreams.

Neither of us said a word for perhaps a half an hour. From my corner, I could see old Dan sitting on the edge of his bunk, eyes half closed, smoking contentedly. Presently he started taking short spasmodic puffs and I waited expectantly. A few long puffs and he began, "You was askin' me t'other day 'bout bass, and since then I've been thinkin' 'bout a fellow that came up here some eight or nine years ago. He was plumb crazy 'bout fishin', and had the dangdest outfit along, you ever did see, little red flies, white ones, brown ones, and all sorts of funny wooden bugs. When I saw it the first time, I asked him what he planned on doin' with all that pile o' jewelry. He laffed and said, he was goin' to show us lumber-jacks how to ketch bass. Well, I'd caught plenty of 'em with frogs and minners and told him so, but never in all my life with such an ornery collection as what he had. Between you and me, I thought he was a little bit off, but told him to go ahead an' see what he could do.

"Then he started askin' me where they was any, and I told him we used to ketch 'em pretty plenty up at Grass Lake, some twenty years ago, when this camp was runnin' logs down the river, but that it hadn't been fished much since.

"Right away this feller gets interested and wants to know where it was. I told him as clost as I could figger, it was 'bout a mile northwest of Bray Lake, an' as far as I knew there wan't no trail. Just the same he was bound to go and stayed with me all that night.

"Well, next mornin' before daylight, he was hittin' the brush an' he didn't come back till just before dark, but dang it all if he didn't have the fines' string o' bass I ever did see. Right then and there, I took back all I'd said about his jewelry. Before he left he gave me a couple o' those bugs an' flies, but I never did get time to try 'em out. One o' those bass he brought in must a'weighed seven pounds if he weighed an ounce."

Then followed a long series of puffs.

"Son," he said after some time, "I'd like to see you go up an' try that lake. They must be some big ones in there yet. In the ole days we had a scow up there an' in the early mornin's, jus' when the mist was risin' off o' the rushes round the aidge, we'd ketch all we could eat with a couple o' frogs before breakfast.

By that time, I was sitting bolt upright on the edge of my bunk, wondering if I was really awake. Imagine having an old timer tell you of a lake that had hardly been fished for twenty years and full of bass up to seven pounds or more. Before I had time to ask him about the location of the lake Dan told me where I'd find a stub of a pencil and an old envelope.

"I'm pretty old and stiff to go up myself but I can tell you pretty close how to get there," he assured me. "Now if you'll gimme your pencil I'll try and draw you a map."

Slowly and laboriously he sketched a rough map on the back of the envelope, then with the stem of his pipe he traced the trail from Bray to Grass Lake.

"Foller up the shore of Bray Lake north from the cabin till you strike a swale, then strike straight northwest for three-quarters of a mile and there you'll find her right in front of you. You can' miss it."

I stowed the map away religiously in my shirt pocket. "That's news to me, Dan," I answered, "and if I don't bring back the brother to that seven pounder tomorrow night, I'll buy you grub for a month."

*Two anglers brace themselves with a stiff drink before the rigorous work of wetting their lines at the Star Fish Camp on Wisconsin's Rice Lake in 1902. (Photograph courtesy of the Minnesota Historical Society)*

We smoked a while longer and talked bass, deer hunting, and game laws, till we were both sleepy and then turned in. I was far too excited to think of sleep, but finally dropped off only to dream of monster black bass striking insanely at every cast. Right in the midst of it, I was awakened by Dan's, "Roll out. Daylight in the swamp."

Breakfast was finished hurriedly, and I plunged into the rain-drenched brush just as daylight was breaking over the east shore of Bray Lake. I might just as well have taken an ice cold shower, for in a minute I was soaked to the skin. I followed Dan's map carefully and in half an hour found myself on a high brushy hill overlooking a tiny alder-fringed lake, not half a mile away. Then followed a mad scramble through some of the densest jumble I had ever seen. The entire slope was burned over and grown up thickly with popple brush and the ground itself, a maze of charred windfalls interlaced with the prickly vines of raspberry. Half the time, I was balanced precariously on downed timber or extricating myself from a network of tangled brush.

Arriving finally at the lake, I found the shore was partly sand and partly mud. All along the edge lay windfalls with inviting bunches of lily pads nestling around their submerged tips. I hit the shore at just such a spot and nervously rigged up my tackle.

While trying to fasten a brown fly to a swivel spinner, I succeeded in running the hook clean through the arm of my shirt. I tried most carefully to back it out, but try as I might, the barb refused to come. It seemed as though I had worked half the morning, before I finally ripped it out in sheer desperation.

Wading out to my waist, so that I could cast without encumbering myself with the whole shoreline, I unlimbered and let the fly sail out toward a bunch of lily pads. It settled gracefully on the edge of a leaf, rested just a second and slipped off. Bang! and a big green form splashed the whole end of the windfall. I let him have it and struck. Yes, I struck and my bedraggled fly came dancing merrily back over the disturbed ripples. I cast again and again, but not another rise did I get. Finally deciding that I must have hooked him pretty badly, I left the windfall and waded up the shore, casting at every likely spot. Some places literally screamed black bass, but no lure I had would bring even a half-hearted strike. By ten o'clock I had fished clear around the lake with only one strike to my record and that the first. I was pretty discouraged and was beginning to think that Old Dan's story was a fizzle or that I

BELOW: *Silhouetted against the morning sunrise, a lone angler makes his initial cast into the Madison River of Yellowstone National Park. (Photograph © Henry H. Holdsworth/Wild By Nature)*

FACING PAGE: *A largemouth bass makes a leap for freedom in an attempt to dislodge the classic Bass-Oreno lure. (Photograph © Doug Stamm/ProPhoto)*

*A boy sets his hook into his breakfast in this circa 1900 oil painting by Philip R. Goodwin. (Courtesy of the Buffalo Bill Historical Center, Cody, Wyoming; gift of Jeffrey F. and Nancy M. Henderson)*

was a no good excuse for a fisherman.

I sat down on a log to think things over, wondering if there wasn't some place I had missed. I did remember one, where the mud had been so soft that I couldn't wade out to east, and had gone back through the alders to the next likely spot. It was half way around the lake, but nevertheless I decided to try it, so back I went, creeping carefully through the brush until I was at the water's edge. The mud was much too soft to hold me, so I stepped on a log lying near, without touching the windfall at whose end I was to cast. It was rather a ticklish place at best, for the brush grew so close to the shore that casting was difficult.

Finding a little opening in the leaves, I tipped my rod back and sailed the fly out over the end of the windfall. It lit gently a few inches from a big lily pad at its very tip. Slap! A boiling swirl of water and the fly started for depths unknown. This time I hooked him firmly and the fight was on. First he dashed for a tangle of half-sunken brush, then just as wildly for the lily pads further out. At every run, I expected to see the line come floating limply to the top. Then down he went and by the fierce, tugging jerks I knew that he was sulking at the bottom. Keeping my balance on the slippery log made it doubly interesting. Once, as I lost my balance, I stepped in up to my knees in the soft ooze and let out ten feet of precious slack while getting back on.

I thought that was the finish but when I recovered my line, he was still on. Finally he seemed to be tiring, so I began to urge him a little, but no sooner did he feel the added pressure, than out he sped again for deep water. Out, out, he went, while the handle whizzed through my fingers. I tried to hold him back, but still the reel screeched. Only a few yards left, when all of a sudden he stopped dead and started to sulk. Here I got in a few yards of slack and thinking he was done for, began to bring him in. This time he changed his tactics. In he rushed straight toward me, while I reeled madly. When about twenty feet away, out of the water he came shaking his head in a last desperate effort. Not once, but three times did he come, making each jump wilder than the one before. All I could do was wind, wind, and keep the tip of my rod down.

The third jump took his last ounce of strength, for after that he came in sullenly. I slipped my hands into his gills and lifted from the water one of the finest bass it has ever been my joy to catch, and one of the best fighters. I laid him down tenderly on a bed of moss and for a long time watched the play of light on the bronze and green of his scales. It was one of those supreme moments that come in the life of every fisherman when he realizes for once, that the big one didn't get away.

After that Grass Lake seemed more cheerful. The sky was bluer and the birds sang more light heartedly than ever. I had solved the mystery and every windfall after that, was cast at not from the water, but from the shore. By late afternoon I had landed two more splendid fish, almost as large as the first and not a one under five pounds.

If I had used a boat, I would have had my limit, but I was more than satisfied. I had discovered a new sport, one as yet unrivaled for me, stalking black bass from the shore. It was almost dark before I reached the cabin at Bray Lake. As I came down the trail Old Dan saw me and yelled, "What luck?"

I answered as unconcernedly as I could, "Oh, I got a few Dan." It seemed as though I never would reach the cabin after that, even though it was only a scant hundred yards away. I did finally arrive however, and with great inward satisfaction spread out my catch for his appraisal.

For a moment he looked at them in silence. "Well I'll be danged," was all he said. "If that fool jewelry ain't turned the trick again."

*A fisherman works the shoreline on the waters of Minnesota's Blackhawk County Park. (Photograph © Richard Hamilton Smith)*

## Alluring Lures

Advertisements for the latest lures liberally peppered the pages of sporting magazines of the first half of the century. Every lure and bait company promised essentially the same thing—more fish and bigger fish— but each company had its own distinctive lure names and creative slogans, each more alluring than the last.

After the 1950s, however, lure ads gradually gave way to ads for trucks, liquor, cigarettes, even underwear. Magazine pages once covered with the names of little bait and lure companies now display the wares of K-Mart, GM, Ford, and Chevrolet. Certainly there are still ads for boats and motors, camping gear, rods and reels, mosquito repellent, and other outdoor equipment in today's sporting magazines, but there is nary a Hula Popper or Dipsy-Doodle to be found.

Fortunately, many small lure companies are alive and well today thanks to a late-twentieth-century advertising venue: the Internet. With a few mouse clicks, the online angler can find a plethora of lures and baits with names such as the Flirty Girty, the Mud Puppy, and the Fat Fighter from companies such as Bass Assassin, Fish Witch, and Mister Twister. They may be online, but their advertising is just as creative and their claims are just as bold as those of their print-and-paper counterparts from forty to seventy-five years ago.

Here are some of the century's most enticing, most creative lure advertisements from their heyday in the first half of the twentieth century.

# HULA POPPER

### "ABSOLUTELY THE BEST TOP WATER PLUG I'VE EVER USED"

—writes E. T. Brown of Haskell, Okla. "The picture shows my fishing buddy Ryland Thomas (right) and me with a string of bass we caught in a small lake near Stigler, Okla., on your Hula Popper. It's the best for casting, for action and for producing the fish."

## BIG NOISE, BIG ACTION GET BIG FISH

Marion Pugh of College Station, Texas, used a Frog Hula Popper to take these Texas whoppers. "The bass ran from 5-1/4 to 2-3/4 lbs. They really go for that surface popping action." Hula Popper obeys your slightest wrist command. You make it pop, plunk, twitch or jerk under perfect control. When at rest colorful rubber Hula Skirt goes into wriggling, squirming action—imitating live bug. Choice of body colors. Casting size (5/8 oz.) or spinning and light tackle size (1/4 oz.)—$1.25 each. Fly-rod size (1/16 oz.)—75c each.

### SURFACE POPPING LURE

HULA POPPER

**FREE**

Fred Arbogast BAITS

16 mm. Color Movies (silent) of sport fishing in U.S. and Canada available without charge for showings to sport clubs. Write for information.

FRED ARBOGAST & CO., INC., 1454 W. North St., Akron 3, Ohio

**WRITE TODAY FOR YOUR BIG FREE COLOR CATALOG—FULL OF PICTURES OF CATCHES**

---

# Hawaiian Wiggler
## Gets Bass

### No. 1 (runs deep) 75c

white, black and white, red and yellow, and solid colors.

(Complete with one rubber skirt.) Extra skirts 15c. Red and black. Easy to change skirts or replace old rubber.

### When She do the Hula Hula

From Ray Drake, Lexington, Ky., "I just returned from Crab Lake, Wis., where your Hawaiian spinner with black and white and red and white skirts caught every kind of fish in the lake. Even the musky and how the walleyes and smallmouth bass went for it. The best part was when one was hooked he always came into the boat and onto the stringer."

### No. 3 Hawaiian Spoon 60c

1 for deep water—No. 3 for shallow.

"The soft rubber legs, all squirming, kill fish that ignore less active baits. You never saw much action till you see my Hawaiians do their dance. Free catalog on request. Sample Offer—Send dollar for two Hawaiians No.

**FRED ARBOGAST,**

**94 North St., Akron, O.**

---

# DILLINGER
## "The Greatest Killer of Them All"

### For both fresh and salt water Game Fish

---

"Fishing with MirrOlures today, I see."

## The Lure with the Built-in FLASH!

# MirrOlures

Send for FREE L & S Fisherman's Log with color "How to Use" insert. Record your fishing trips. Learn which L & S lure to use, and when.

L & S BAIT CO., INC. Bradley 35, Illinois

---

# "gurglehead"

a Trenton lure

$1.25 See your tackle dealer

TRENTON MFG. CO.
COVINGTON, KY.

---

# REWARD
## Bayou Boogie TWINS

UNDERWATER

TOPPER

This murderous pair are wanted everywhere for **FISH SNATCHING! THEY WORK IN PAIRS!** Fish working on water surface, Topper grabs them. His actions fool all fish as he 'pops' on the surface...on retrieve, belly roll, swims, dives a few inches under water like a frantic minnow!

Bayou Boogie Underwater gets those big ones **DOWN DEEP**...amazing antics trick fish on to his hooks every time.

### SPIN — CAST — TROLL

With both—they're equal to an entire tackle box of ordinary lures! We dare you to try this. Take the Bayou Boogie twins, 'Topper' and 'Underwater' on your next fishing trip (no tackle box)...you'll out-fish your buddies on top of the water or under water for all kinds of fish. Buy 'em by the pair..$1.25 ea.

Get your 'Bayou Boogie' Twins at your dealer

**Write today for FREE full color catalog**

**A. D. MFG. CO.**

1917 CHOUTEAU AVE. St. Louis, Mo.

---

BIG FISH SMACK

## THE HUSKY IKE

It's the HUSKY IKE for husky fish... biggest of the LAZY IKE family. A perfect caster. Excellent Troller. Tantalizing minnow action. Floats when stationary—goes down to 5 feet on fast retrieve, 3½″ long, weighs ⅝ oz. Anglers everywhere call it a killer on Muskies and Northerns—a honey for big Bass and Trout. Your favorite dealer sells Lazy Ikes.

**FREE CATALOG TELLS YOU HOW—WRITE FOR IT**

Husky Ikes $1.40 ea.

**Kautzky's LAZY IKE CO., Dept. F4, Fort Dodge, Iowa**

# 1928

# FISHERMAN'S LUCK

## By Lou J. Eppinger

This humorous "letter" was published in 1928 as a booklet by the Eppinger fishing lure manufacturer to promote the firm to anglers everywhere. While the essay is signed by Fred F. Henkel, fishing book collectors remain unclear if there really was a Fred Henkel, or if the story was written by an unsung marketing genius with a golden pen; it was in fact copyrighted in Lou J. Eppinger's name. In the end, the lost history of this tidbit of fishing lore simply adds to the piece's charm.

It is known, however, that Eppinger's lures have won a special place in anglers' tackleboxes. The company dates back to 1906, when Lou Eppinger developed a special spoon that became the forerunner of what may be the most famous lure of all time, the Dardevle. The name paid tribute to the U.S. Marines of World War I, nicknamed the "Devil Dogs" by the Germans; a chaste Eppinger changed the spelling of "devil" because he didn't like seeing the word in print.

What is also common knowledge is that while Eppinger's Dardevle sometimes seems to be almost magical in its ability to lure fish, an angler also needs luck, as detailed in this quaint history of one man's monumental efforts to catch fish.

*This lucky man's dinner will begin with a nice fresh fish appetizer, followed by a succulent fish entree with a tasty dish of fish on the side. Would you like a fish soup or fish salad with that, sir? (Photograph courtesy of the Jackson Hole Historical Society & Museum)*

THIS IS A sketch of my fishing experiences. It all started about thirty-three years ago. I was a kid of ten then, and I've been at it ever since. At first I had to go along with the older ones. Then we used a drop line. Used to go to the Hackensack River. When we got a little older we were allowed to go by ourselves to the near by ice ponds and clay pits. We used to catch yellow perch, catfish and bass.

## BIRCH POLE DAYS

The very first equipment I had was a birch pole. My Dad cut it for me. A piece of wrapping string and a penny's worth of ring hooks (they were five for a penny in those days) and a cork from an old bottle completed the necessary outfit. Well, they were the good old days. I guess there's many a grown up man can look back and remember birch pole days. And maybe, he'd be willing to trade even just to have them back. A fellow could go out then and in an hour get a real mess.

## THE STORE POLE

It wasn't so long, but it seemed like ages, before we graduated from the birch pole class to the long Bamboo stage. We used to buy them at the store for fifteen cents. I always picked out the longest one in the bunch, it didn't cost any more. We felt pretty smart with our store poles, using sun-fish belly and skitter for bass. Sometimes we would get a big fellow on a worm. Half of the time the bass would land up in a tree with the tip of the pole and the line all tangled galley west. We used to horse them over our heads and then spend an hour in getting them untangled.

Yes, sir. Them was the good old days. But, by the time we got into the split bamboo class and thought ourselves real anglers, the waters in them parts was pretty well fished out. We were sure proud of the store poles and bought a floater, or a dobber, as we used to call them in those days. But it didn't matter. If they ain't no fish, no pole or rod, or no kind of fancy tackle will catch them.

## DISCOURAGED?—NO!

It's been about six years now since I fished in my native waters. Just ain't no use in wasting good time and bait. I've got to travel over to New York State now when I feel the urge a coming on. And it's getting to be the same at a lot of the New York lakes that I've been fishing. I come home on Sunday with the tackle and a grouch but darn few fish. You see I have to do most of my fishing on Sundays.

I thought that maybe it was the bait. I tried pork rind and got a few small pickerel. You see I had always been a worm fisherman and I couldn't get much satisfaction out of pork rind. And I tried feather spinners and a lot of other contraptions, but none of them gave me much satisfaction.

LEFT: *The cover of the boxed edition of "Fisherman's Luck," a 1928 promotional book from Eppinger's lure company.*

FACING PAGE: *A walleye flashes its sharp teeth just before it strikes a lure. (Photograph © Doug Stamm/ProPhoto)*

OVERLEAF: *Two fisherman try their luck in Minnesota's Mantrap Lake. (Photograph © Richard Hamilton Smith)*

## READY TO QUIT?—MAYBE!

Well Sir—Mr. Eppinger, I was about through last June. Just about ready to quit and go in for golf or regular Sunday picnicking. I didn't want to do it. This fishing germ gets in the blood and it stays. But I was getting pretty darn disgusted with it all.

## HOPES AROUSED

I was reading one of the fishing magazines on a Sunday. It was the second Sunday in June, and I read an advertisement about how I could get a big assortment of fancy fishing tackle for five dollars. I wrote them a letter and sent along a new five dollar bill. I made up my mind it was the last five bucks that I was going to shoot, and if my luck did not change I was going to lay-off of fishing for good.

Well they sent me the assortment. There was a lot of plugs. One little jointed affair that looked so darn much like a fish that I was sure it would keep me busy unloading my hook. I couldn't wait for Sunday to come. And when it finally did drag around, I was up bright and early a heading for my favorite lake about thirty-five

miles east of home. I guess the wife and kids thought I was crazy getting them up before six, rounding up things and packing them in the little Chev. They were still half asleep when I shoved off—with visions of a great day's catch.

Well I hired a boat as soon as I got to the edge of the lake. I was pretty sure that I'd need it. You see I was figuring on getting a barrel of fish with all my doo-dads that I had to use.

## EXPERIMENTING

I started out with one of the plugs first. I kept the darn thing in the water according to directions for nearly three hours and not a bite. Not a darn nibble. I went back to worms and put one on my hook, spitting on it three times for luck. You can imagine that I was pretty darn disgusted. I caught one perch. Then they quit biting. I was pretty darn disgusted all right. I hauled in the boat and then started my old method of fishing from the shore. I tried the plug again in some of the old holes where I had caught both pickerel and bass. But not a bit of action. I was madder than a wet hen. I was ready to swear off fishing forever.

## MEETS THE "OLD BOY" HIMSELF

I was just getting all the junk together to throw it in the lake when I spied a Dardevle in the tackle box that had come with the other lures. I was just about to throw it all in the drink, when something stopped me. I don't know how I come to keep the Dardevle. Cause when it came with the other stuff, I said to my wife. "What good is that dam thing? There ain't no fish that's dumb enough or that foolish that he'll go after that." But, my wife is Scotch. She laughed and said keep it. Maybe it would come in all right for a can opener when I was out fishing or we might use it some time to repair the Chev.

## BEING KIDDED

My wife's a funny woman, she gets a kick out of going along with me and sitting on the bank. When she ain't playing with the kids or thinking about the dishes she left in the sink, she's always kidding me. I guess all women are just natural born kidders. She's kind of got

*"Good Fishing! Starts at Eppinger's" proclaims the cover of this classic 1930s brochure showing the firm's famous Dardevle line.*

*Alluring lure boxes: Some lure boxes were better at catching anglers than the lures inside were at catching fish. The sales slogan that wins the day—although who can remember how many fish the lure actually caught—is that for the Scandinavian Sockaroo from the Scandinavian Bait Company of Stillwater, Minnesota: "The bait with plenty of vim, vigor and viggle." Memorabilia owner: Pete Press. (Photograph © Howard Lambert)*

used to my swearing when I get a pork rind on wrong or get a back lash, or get caught in a snag. She saw me looking at that Dardevle, and I could see a smile start over her face. She didn't say a word but that smile meant a thousand words. I was being kidded. I guess that's what made me determine to try the miniature Ford fender. I didn't have much faith. It was getting late and about time to start home. I remembered reading about what luck the other fellows had had with them, but it sounded like the old bunk to me. You see it only goes to prove when you think you know it all, you are just about getting lined up to learn another little lesson.

## DISCOVERY

Well I put the darn thing on the line. I shortened my telescope pole to about four and a half feet—and I made a cast. Just as the Old Boy hit the water and started that swimming motion—a big pickerel made a strike and say—he went for it. But the son-of-a-gun spit it out. Well—I couldn't get him to try it again. It was getting late and the kids were getting kind of fretful, and the Missus said we better call it a day. So we began to burn the gas, going west with the sun toward home.

## ANTICIPATION

All the way home I was making plans in my mind for the next Sunday. I was sure going to give Dardevle a chance. So when Sunday rolled around I was all set up and ready for business at another favorite lake. I fetched in two beauties in a little while—one was 16½ inches and the other one was a little over 18 inches. This was late in July and I went every Sunday regular until October and altogether I pulled out twenty-four pickerel. They wasn't all on Dardevle but they was all on members of the Dardevle family. They were all on your baits.

## REALIZATION

I got enthusiastic after pulling in that first one. You can imagine how I felt. I just made up my mind right then and there that I'd apologize to you some day and I guess this is that apology. I went to my dealer after that first Sunday and he only had two left. They are Dardevlets. One was a red one with a green stripe, this is my favorite, and the other was a black one with a white chunk. I lost the black and white one after a few casts, but I still got the red and green one. I travelled all the way over to Paterson, N. J., and got some more there. The dealer there didn't have a big stock. It seemed that everybody had gone Dardevle crazy and the Dealers had had a big run so that the back end of the season left them pretty well cleaned out. I hadn't much casting experience, so I began practicing every chance I had. I soon made up for this deficiency and now I guess I'm about as proficient as anybody in these parts. My wife gave me a good back-lash reel, she ordered from your catalog for my birthday present and with that Baby I sure can put the "Old Boy" just about where I want him to go. And, if there's any fish in the neighborhood—we eat fish.

## THE "OLD BOY" PROVES HIMSELF

The last day of the season I got my biggest catch. It was a 19½ inch pickerel and a beauty. You'd have been proud to have landed him yourself. I raised him three times before I could get him really interested. I couldn't get him to take hold of the bait.

Finally I got some grease off the car springs of the Chevrolet and gave the Old Boy a few dabs here and there and then went after him again. Say, that tussle that fellow gave me, it'd make a great slow motion movie. When we were first introduced I was standing on a rock about ten feet from shore, just with shoes on, I had to hop, skip, run and jump over rocks, fallen logs and land him through brush over a lot of debris. He sure gave some fight before he was landed and ready to call it quits.

From my experience I find that by reeling in with jerks gives the best results. It allows the Dardevle to sink for a fraction of a second and then it starts again on an erratic swimming motion, just like a wounded fish will do. This has a lot of advantages over reeling in on a slow even motion to my way of thinking.

## A REGULAR FELLOW

I believe in being a true sportsman. I never take more than I can use. Always try to leave some for the other fellow and the next time. I never like to fish where

*"Patience is a virtue," an anxious fisherman reminds himself, as he watches a fish investigate his lure. (Photograph © Jack Bissell)*

*"There is certainly something in angling
. . . that tends to produce a gentleness of
spirit, and a pure serenity of mind." —
Washington Irving, "The Angler" from*
The Sketch-Book *(Photograph ©
Richard Hamilton Smith)*

another fellow is fishing. Last Sunday—I was out and several others were fishing and using plugs. When I asked them what luck they were having they said that the fish wouldn't bite. Then I asked if they cared if I'd make a few casts where they were fishing. They invited me to go ahead. So I shot out the old red and green baby, my favorite one, as I said before. No sooner out to water than I got a raise out of a pickerel. It didn't take long to land him and he measured fourteen and a half inches. Those fellows were sure surprised. They asked me what kind of bait I was using and I told them it was Lou Eppinger's Dardevlet. They wanted to know how long I'd been using it, how much it cost, where they could get one—maybe they wasn't converted right then and there. Seeing is believing.

## SHOWING OFF

One of my old friends fishing right by my side one Sunday evening was using a plug. He hadn't got a thing all evening, while I pulled out three with my little old red and green Dardevlet, all between twelve and fourteen inches, in less than an hour. The following Sunday he went along again, but didn't have the courage to try his luck. He just sat in the car. Said he'd rather watch me. He got a kick out of seeing me cast and reeling them in. He's an addict too, now—and I could name a lot of boys that got the same thrill out of discovering the Old Dardevle family just the same as I did

I lost four Dardevlets last season. But, say, it was worth it. I sure got a lot of sport out of them before they disappeared. I still got four left—and you can bet your sweet life that I'll have a good supply on hand next season if I have to walk all the way to Detroit to get them. Yours till they ain't no more fish—and thanking you for putting a real kick back in one fisherman's fishing.

Yours sincerely,
Fred F. Henkel

LEFT: *A circa 1940s magazine ad extols the virtues of Eppinger lures.*

FACING PAGE: *Anglers silhouetted against the setting sun as they fish during the "magic hour." (Photograph © Bill Marchel)*

# THE NORTHERN PIKE

By O. Warren Smith

O. Warren Smith was a fisherman and a preacher, both callings that he came by naturally. On his father's side was a long lineage of pioneers, hunters, and trappers; on his mother's, an equally lengthy line of preachers and clergymen.

Along with serving in many churches in his native Wisconsin, Smith also worked as the fishing editor for *Outdoor Life* and several other classic angling magazines. He compiled his vast knowledge of fishing lore into numerous volumes packed with time-tested tips and techniques.

This essay on stalking the northern pike is part of *Angling Success* (1935), an anthology of tips and techniques penned by the best and brightest anglers of the day. Smith's article is redolent of the era's style of outdoors writing, blending how-to advice with purple prose eulogizing the great endeavor that is fishing.

*An angry northern pike leaps from the water, fighting to spit out the spinner that has snagged it. (Photograph © Doug Stamm/ProPhoto)*

THERE IS NO more interesting group of fishes than the true pikes, from the little river pickerel up to the lordly muskellunge himself. In passing, allow me to emphasize the fact that the much execrated pickerel is as true a pike as is the muskellunge. Lying between the two extremes, we find the subject of this chapter, the great northern pike. Before we go on to discuss this *wasser wolf*, suffer a word or two concerning the much mooted "pike question."

Surely every reader of outdoor periodicals and angling literature knows that the so-called wall-eyed pike is not a pike at all, but belongs to the perch family—is simply a big perch. Just compare him with the common yellow perch and you will understand, without going into the matter of scientific differences with their jaw-breaking nomenclature. The pike family, as I have already said, consists of the small pickerels, the great pike or great northern pike, and the muskellunge. The little pickerel does not develop into a northern pike any more than a northern pike develops into a muskellunge. For the most part, pickerel are small fish, while the northern pike sometimes rivals the muskellunge himself in size and weight, and, to my way of thinking, is the equal of the latter in fighting ability.

Surely it is hardly necessary today to spend much time explaining the differences between the three groups of pikes, so much has been written upon the subject; but a word or two, divorced of all scientific terms and phraseology, may be advantageous. Of course my readers know that color and marking are never safe guides in classifying fish, depending as they do upon food and environment. We must seize upon some anatomical differences which are constant. While there are several "anatomical differences" between the three groups mentioned, I mention but one—always present and easily read once you have trained the eye a bit. The cheek and gill-cover of the pickerel are always both fully scaled; the cheek of the great northern pike is fully scaled, while the gill-cover is scaled on the upper half only; and the muskellunge has both cheek and gill cover scaled only on the upper halves. As I have said, there are other anatomical differences, but this one fact is sufficient. Disabuse your mind of all arguments concerning color, body form, etc., and stick this one difference in the back chambers of your mind.

There has been much written regarding the supe-

*"Great sport fishing here" reads the rather understated caption on this 1910 "tall-tale" postcard. The three anglers appear to be no match for the northern pike attacking their rods and reels. (Courtesy Roger Welsch)*

riority of the 'lunge as a fighter over other members of the family—a matter with which I am far from being in agreement. To my way of thinking, after a lifetime of fishing, given two fish of equal weight, and in the same environment, there is not the slightest difference in their fighting qualities. I had just as soon try conclusions with a fifteen pound northern pike as a fifteen pound muskellunge; and when you are hitched up to a thirty pound northern pike, I am here to tell you that you are hitched up with thirty pounds of as great ichthyic trouble as ever flirted a caudal fin in the face of a chagrined and disappointed angler. I know that many will not agree with me, which is neither here nor there; I am only giving my own convictions. Just because a northern pike to some people is "nothing but a pickerel" is no reason why I should contemptuously turn down one of our most satisfactory ichthyic battlers.

Naturally, much depends upon the character of a fish's habitat, and the temperature and character of the water.

Cold, clear water seems to pep up a fish, even as man is invigorated by a bracing climate. Then, too, one should never expect best results from a fish unless proper tackle is employed. I have written quite largely upon the joys of fly fishing for sunfish, using proper paraphernalia. So in fishing for northern pike, do not anticipate great sport when hand-lines and "shark tackle" are employed. I know I am too apt to err on the side of lightness when it comes to rods, though I always employ a line strong enough to prevent, if possible, a fish's escaping with a mouth full of steel. I do not sleep well when I know that a northern pike is somewhere in the lake fighting desperately to rid itself of a plug. No, line and gimp should be stout enough to hold any northern pike, however light the rod may be.

Probably there is no better rod for northern pike fishing than the regulation casting rod, say 5½ feet long, built rather thick in the waist. I have used a 6½ footer with delight, but it is too long for general use; too liable to smash under heavy strain such as a goodly northern pike can exert. I want the reel to be a 100 yard double multiplying one, with the level-wind attachment. The line should be new, 20 or 30-pound-test. Note I said new. An old line is always a danger, for one rotten spot may lose the best fish. As to terminal tackle . . . well, that all depends upon the method of angling

to be employed. And as every angler at all versed in the sport knows, there are many methods used—from the simple hand-line to the fly rod, yes, *the fly rod*.

The first northern pike fishing I ever witnessed—I was too small to do more than accompany the fisherman—was with a heavy hand-line, to which were attached a number of lead weights and a big spoon. The weighted line was swung about the head in ever widening circles until considerable momentum was achieved, then suddenly released and the spoon flung far from the boat. The line was recovered hand over hand, and sometimes, quite often, for this was before our waters were fished out, a northern pike would take hold of the spoon. There is not much to recommend this sport today, though considerable skill was required to properly cast the lure. I doubt if it would prove overly remunerative nowadays.

Trolling is probably the most popular method employed for taking northern pike, and by and large perhaps the most uniformly successful, although of that I am not as certain as are many of my contemporaries. In trolling I use, and strongly advise, the short casting rod already mentioned, in your favorite material and make. Undoubtedly, the best spoon is the old-fashioned fluted or even kidney-shaped. The spoon must be well made and strong, and should be attached to the line with a six or eight inch wire gimp, for the northern pike, in common with all members of the family, has the disagreeable habit of "striking over" and his sharp teeth will sever the best of lines as easily as will a knife. We often read of northern pike turning and deliberately seizing the line in its mouth and so liberating itself. Well, when it happens it is not because the fish has figured the matter out; only by accident does the line get between its teeth. Enough to remember that the fish carries a pair of good "wire cutters," as it were, and keep the silk from them.

While I am a "go alone" fisherman, in trolling there is a very real advantage in having a companion. I do not mean a boatman, a guide, but another angler—then fish turn and turn about. If going alone a rod-holder is almost a necessity, for a rod sticking out over the stern of the boat may be pulled overboard before the fisherman can reach it. Lines do snarl, you know. The secret of successful trolling, given a good water and fish, lies in slow movement. I discovered early

*The first morning light usually signals the start of a fishing day, but this pair of anglers is already trolling the waters of Minnesota's Elbow Lake as the sun comes up. (Photograph © Richard Hamilton Smith)*

in my angling life that I was apt to take fish when coming about, so I figured that it was because the spoon was slowed up. Acting upon the principle, I began slow fishing, and lo, I took more fish. Drop the spoon down, well down, and move as slowly as you can. Of course, there are places and places to troll; that I need not say. One must know where fish feed and work there, though northern pike are great roamers and may be taken almost anywhere. Just the same, deep water off a weed bed or sand bar, where the hungry water wolves wait for minnows, is always a likely spot. The northern pike loves to lie concealed in lily pads or grass, ready to dash upon a hapless, helpless minnow, frog, or anything that can minister in the least to his voracious appetite. It takes a great many pounds of lesser fish to make one 20 pound northern pike.

I do not know but that this is as good a place as any to mention the important matter of playing and gaffing, which holds true whatever the method of taking. A northern pike has a vast amount of staying power, differing of course in individuals. I have played a ten-pounder for twenty minutes, only to bring him to net at the end of the period protestingly; and I have vanquished a fifteen-pounder in half the time. By and large, though, the larger the fish the greater the problem. Play the fish as long as he wants to fight. More northern pike are lost because the angler was in too great haste to use the net or gaff. That last ounce of strength, manifesting itself in a sudden convulsive plunge, may spell disaster. A gaff is better than a net, for it is next to impossible to get one of the latter strong enough to lift in a twenty-pounder. A pike net should be deep, deeper than the length of any possible fish. As I said, a strong gaff is better, but do not undertake to gaff a large northern pike without first having administered a sharp blow on the head with a club, or having sent a pellet of lead between the eyes from a thirty-two revolver. I do not like shooting fish, but a large northern pike requires a dose of that medicine. Beware the convulsive plunge when the shot is administered. Here is the secret of successful landing: play to exhaustion, then stun before gaffing.

A more enjoyable method, although I am not altogether sure a more successful, is casting. Now casting calls for more skill, tackle skill, and understanding of the fish's ways. Everything heretofore said of tackle is

*A classic boat awaits another fishing trip on a quiet afternoon in Quebec, Canada. (Photograph © Stephen Kirkpatrick)*

*A lean, mean northern pike stops its frenzied thrashing just long enough for the angler to scoop it up with the net. (Photograph © Doug Stamm/ProPhoto)*

reëmphasized. Do not forget that I mentioned the importance of a level-wind reel and new line; the latter for strength, the former for convenience. The angler will be so busy playing his fish—always granted he hooks one—that he will have no time to lay the line on the spool, a matter of first importance. Two-thirds of our back-lashes are the result of faulty spooling. For casting, I must have some action in the rod, though remembering the vital importance of backbone. A finger-hook is also essential requisite. To throw a rod from your hand, or have it jerked away by an especially obstreperous northern pike is tragedy indeed, tragedy magnified! I speak from experience.

As to the lure, much will depend upon the particular angler's idiocrasy. It is woefully hazardous to recommend any particular spoon or lure, for someone is certain to know from experience that it is no good, not to mention the jealous lure-maker whose lures are not mentioned. I have a well-known predilection for a white and red lure, having found those colors in combination most attractive. I have one old lure, *once* red and white, which was very attractive, and still is a fish-taker though its colors are well faded. The hooks need to be fastened securely, not merely screwed into the wood of the lure. I used to be an advocate of the single hook, but of late years I have changed to trebles, finding that too often I missed hooking my best fish with the single hook. Where we are employing the cigar, or minnow-shaped lure, it seems almost essential that we have trebles. I used to bemoan too well hooked fish, but of late years my moans have been for fish not hooked. I require two trebles today. If a northern pike is not hooked at the first mad attack, he is quick to discover the fraud, and lo, he does not put up a fight, much less come to gaff.

What was heretofore said regarding the natural hang-outs of northern pike still obtains, of course, though the method of the caster differs somewhat from that of the troller. Here the fisherman does the major part of the work; in trolling it is the boatman who labors. One must know his casting reach and general ability with short rod and multiplying reel. While it is never wisdom to strain the cast, it is wisdom to cast as far as possible with absolute control. The northern pike is a much shyer fish than he is sometimes credited with being. The shadow of a boat, or the flash of a swinging rod, is enough to cause him to settle back in the reeds or deep down in the water. One must cast circumspectly and with intimate understanding of the whims of the fish he seeks. There can be no crass work, nor room for luck, where the shy northern pike is concerned. Of course in Canada, where the fish has not learned the full meaning of a bouncing lure, the situation is different. Which leads me to say that the northern pike is the same fish in the United States that he is in Canada, though much more numerous in the latter country.

The boat should slip along quietly, and with as little commotion as possible, out beyond the weed beds, mouths of incoming streams, or grass borders, where the hungry fellows lie in wait for frogs, minnows, or whatever moves. I know they will not refuse a mouse or young muskrat. Now to drop, no, *slip* the lure right into his feeding ground, letting it sink a bit before beginning to reel, is almost sure to secure a strike, unless the work has been done so crudely that the fish has become alarmed. Do not try to cover too much territory, but fish carefully as you go, remembering the golden rule of all angling: do not over fish. The best hours for casting are early morning and again at evening, the half-lights being conducive to catches. There is such a thing as a pike day—the hot, close, mizzling day that arrives in mid-summer now and then.

All fish, especially northern pike, are stirred by a great hunger or unreasonable desire to hunt. I have taken a half-dozen good fish in a couple of hours under such conditions. It is better to have the surface of the water roughened than glassy, for under the first condition the fish's visibility, from its view-point, is impaired; though too rough water is not conducive to expert casting, a dancing boat destroying aim and rendering distances deceptive.

Speaking of rough water naturally suggests live-bait fishing. Successful fishing for northern pike with live bait calls for a day when the winds cuff the waves until they foam with rage. (I am speaking of small lakes, and not Lake Superior where considerable northern pike fishing has been done.) Now this whole matter of live-bait fishing calls for much discussion, so many anglers frowning upon it as "unsportsmanlike." Drat the word! I cannot take time to enter into the question fully here, but I cannot see why live-bait fishing is not just as legitimate as casting a lure, or trolling, providing the angler himself is a true sportsman. I do know there are days when a large minnow or small fish will result in great sport, and a record breaker.

I do not vary my outfit one iota from that I employ in casting, though some of my friends insist that a long cane pole, equipped with guide and reel-seat, is the proper thing. I grant its convenience and general efficiency, but I cling tenaciously to my short casting rod, casting no aspersions upon the cane-pole users. It is not so much your tackle as you that matters in sportsmanship. But to return. A windy day, especially along in September, when the whitecaps are rolling and the water is being thoroughly stirred, seems somehow to augment the northern pike's appetite, and set him roaming in quest of food, lots of food. One requires a good sturdy boat—one to be depended upon,—a heavy anchor, and a length of rope. Anchored off a weed bed, in a thoroughfare between two lakes, at the edge of the channel, or in some other known feeding ground, the piker is ready for business.

Now the bait. I have studied this question for these many years, being as much interested in the northern pike's likes and dislikes—habits if you will—as in successfully taking him. I am fully satisfied that there is nothing quite so tasty to a northern pike's palate as a medium sized sucker, say 8 or 10 inches long. It may be imagination on my part, but I am firmly convinced in my own mind that the fish has an especial liking for the sucker, though I do not want you to ask me why. Second to the sucker is the ordinary chub. For such fishing the bait can be large, though a 10 inch sucker is difficult to properly fasten to the hook unless an especially large steel is employed. I use two hooks, the double bait hook, lacking which I make one for myself, simply extending a second hook from the first by means of wire gimp and thrusting the steel through the body of the minnow, well back. Sometimes I use a float, though I much prefer not, interfering as it does with the action of the game. I like to hold my own line, have the thrill of feeling the first onslaught of the hungry northerner. One must fish deep and compose his soul with patience. I know one or two bays along Lake Superior's southern shore where on a proper day one can have sport supreme, and maybe catch a record breaking northern pike. Do not frown too much upon live-bait

fishing until you have explored its mysteries and enjoyed its possibilities.

We have discussed trolling, casting, and live-bait fishing; the three, shall I say, orthodox methods of taking northern pike. But there remains another method not so well known one not often written about because not often practiced. I refer to fly fishing. Yes, northern pike can be taken on artificial flies, though the fly fishing is not much like the sport as we commonly conceive of it—*i.e.,* capturing small-mouth bass and the various species of trout. Perhaps more skill, or at least skill of an entirely different variety, is called for. We must admit at once that the fish is not what we commonly regard as a fly fish, a fish which naturally feeds upon various forms of insect life. The very fact that the method is somewhat unusual and original commends it to the discriminating angler. I think anyone at all familiar with the northern pike will readily admit that an *Esox lucius* weighing anywhere from 3 to 15 pounds would give a good account of himself on the end of a fly rod. If I were weaving yarns, I might spin one concerning an 18-pounder on an 8-ounce fly rod; but as that was a hazardous experiment with a tragic ending, I will not weary the reader with the narrative. Anglers as a rule do not like to tell of defeat and smashed tackle, and I am no exception to the rule.

Naturally, tackle for such fishing, especially if the angler plans or expects to connect up with a large fish, must be of the best; in any event, whatever the size of northern pike, the rod and line must be stiff and stout. I am employing a heavy trout rod, or shall I say a light salmon rod? My chosen tool at present is a 9½-foot split-bamboo, weighing in the neighborhood of 12 ounces. It is none too heavy. I do not recommend so *light* a rod for heavy northern pike. This much the would-be pike fly fisherman must bear in mind: he is going up against a weighty and resourceful fish, more resourceful than the lure caster realizes. Given a fly rod, the odds are all on the pike's end of the argument, especially if weighing anywhere above five pounds.

The reel must be large, for 100 yards of 20-pound-test line is none too much nor too strong. I would err on the side of a bit stronger line rather than a lighter. I prefer a large single action reel, after the ilk of salmon reels, yet I can conceive of an automatic as almost ideal, though one will have to watch the game

*This colorful collection of lures hails from one of the most famous plug manufacturer of the twentieth century—the James Heddon and Sons company of Dowagiac, Michigan. Legend has it that one day James Heddon was waiting for a fishing friend on the shore of a lake. To while away the time, he whittled on a chunk of wood and then threw his carving into the lake's waters—where a big bass attacked it. This episode sparked the idea of carving wooden lures (and inspired the later name "plug"), which were first offered commercially by Heddon in 1901. On the line here is a rare frogskin-patterned, propped Spin-Diver, made from 1918 to 1926. Memorabilia owner: Northland Fishing Museum of Osseo, Wisconsin. (Photograph © Howard Lambert)*

closely and handle his reel cleverly. What has been said before concerning the necessity of a wire gimp or leader, applies here with increased force. A warning every variety of northern pike angler should bear in mind is, beware the fish's razor-like teeth; not only will they sever a line as easily as a sharp knife, but they will also rip an angler's fingers with all the painful effects of an angered wildcat's poisonous claws. Referring again to the reel, I have used large sized single action casting reels, like the "Winona," with considerable success. You must be able to retrieve line quickly and easily.

When it comes to the artificial flies, we are all at sea. There are just no northern pike flies on the market; of course not, and I doubt if there will ever be. I have found a large buck-tail, sometimes the haired treble from an ordinary spoon-hook, can be made to serve.

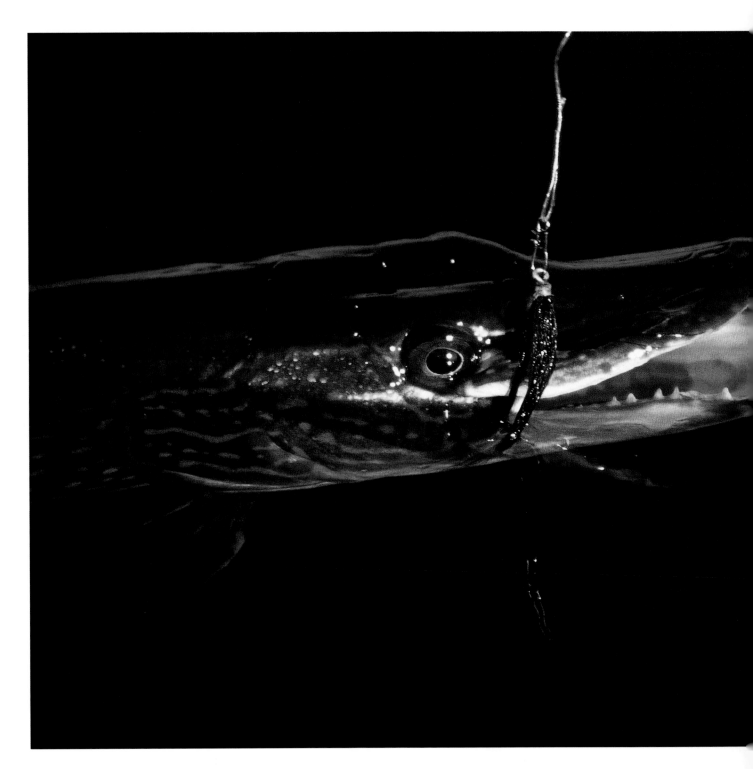

Better tie, or have tied, a sprawly, scraggly buck-tail, the more "splatter-wise" in form the better—*i.e.,* the more alluring. I have used regular salmon flies with fairly good results, although I have had difficulty in hooking the fish. As I think was pointed out under the discussion of lures, it seems that a treble is required to effectually penetrate the armor-plate mouth of his honor, *Esox lucius.* It is rare fun to tie your own flies, striving

to secure something that will attract the attention of this preternaturally shy fish.

I cannot add much to the method of fly fishing for northern pike, for I am only experimenting. I am employing what may be designated as a modified black bass method—casting towards known hang-outs of the moody gentlemen, and jerking the lure to create as much commotion as possible; then, if nothing happens, I allow the lure to settle two or more inches beneath the surface and retrieve it with spasmodic motions, or jerks, opening and closing the hairs. When the center of the "fly" is built of red feathers, the opening and closing of the buck-tail makes an arresting lure. Fortunately for the ambitions of the would-be northern pike fly-fisher, the long-nosed fellow is not overly particular as to pattern, so long as it is active enough to convince him that the thing is sufficient to fill an aching void. Once the fish is firmly hooked, if a good one, the trouble and the sport begin, and for the life of me I am not sure as to whether it is trouble or sport.

As undoubtedly the reader knows, *Esox lucius* is found the world 'round, save perhaps in Spain and Portugal, Greenland, and Iceland, although it is found in streams flowing into the Arctic Ocean and Hudson Bay. As I have already said or intimated, it is found in the Great Lakes and confluents, and of course in the St. Lawrence River. From the Atlantic Seaboard to the western edge of the Great Plains, it is a well known fish, although usually called "pickerel." Perhaps the upper Ohio Valley, the Mississippi Valley, and the Valley of the St. Lawrence afford the best fishing. It has not had its just due at the hands of anglers, for they have thought of it as the "pickerel," or "river snake," although usually I think the fish so designated is another species. However, a northern pike must sometime in its life be small, so unless one stops to examine each capture, a "pickerel" well may be a small northern pike. Given room and plenty of food, an *Esox lucius* develops alder-manic proportions, and becomes a foeman worthy of any angler's steel.

*At the end of a long battle, an exhausted northern pike is reeled in. (Photograph © Dale C. Spartas/The Green Agency)*

# The Rods and Reels That Made History

Once upon a time during all of our childhoods, kite string tied to a branch with a penny hook on the end was the hot item for angling with the gang down at the old fishing hole. When we got that first store-bought rod and reel, suddenly the world was never the same again.

This selection of ads highlight some of the rods and reels that won our hearts and caught the big ones in the early part of the century.

# THE KITCHEN=SINK FISH

## By Gordon MacQuarrie

Gordon MacQuarrie (1900–1956) was best known for his series of humorous sport-ing stories relating the comings and goings of the Old Duck Hunters' Association. The Old Duck Hunters were fictitious but based in fact: MacQuarrie's father-in-law was Al Peck, a Superior, Wisconsin, automobile dealer who served as the model for that lovable rapscallion, the Old Man, more respectfully known as the President of the Association. And in the chronicles of the group's doings, most hunters and anglers could see something of themselves and their sporting friends.

MacQuarrie was a journalist by trade, working for the Superior *Evening Telegram* before moving on to the Milwaukee *Journal*, where he served for more than two decades as the outdoors editor. His series about the Old Duck Hunters' Association and his other outdoors articles appeared in a variety of national sporting magazines.

This story is classic MacQuarrie. As with many of his pieces about the Old Duck Hunters, it is often less a battle between man and nature, and more of a bonfire of human vanities.

*Flies, a rod, a reel, a spare cigar, and a warming drink—everything an angler needs for a long, satisfying day in the stream. (Photograph © Bill Buckley/The Green Agency)*

IN THE MONTH of May, when spring is a blessed fact in most places, churlish Lake Superior declines to be a good neighbor. This greatest of fresh-water bodies hangs on to departing winter by its coat-tails, fights hard to keep its vast ice-fields from withering before the prairie winds. Some days the westerly winds drive the ice-floes beyond sight of land. Then the wind shifts, and back come the chalk-white rafts to jam the bays and harbors and river mouths. When the lake wind is king, its cold will be felt some distance inland.

A strange climate, this. Raw winter in control on the lake shore many a day when, fifteen miles inland, the country is soaking up 70- and 80-degree warmth. At least one newspaper in a lake-shore city has acknowledged this whimsical weather by publishing, daily in spring, the temperature not only of the city but of the interior at a point thirty miles away. Thus lake dwellers learn when they may escape the cold wind in a game of golf, a country ride—or a bit of fishing.

Now, coursing down for sixty-six miles to the south shore of this chilly old lake is the river Brule. Early in the season this estimable front stream may, in its upper reaches, soak in 90 degrees, while down below, near the lake, the Brule runs through temperatures of 45 or 50 degrees.

Strange things can happen to a fisherman in Maytime along this storied Wisconsin stream. A man can fish it of a morning near the lake and see ice form in his rod guides. Later, hunting the sun, he can drive to an upper river put-in and get his neck thoroughly sunburned, and wish to high heaven he had left off the long underwear.

You who fish it—and every troutster hopes he will—should be forewarned so that you may come with clothing appropriate both for late winter and full summer. The only solution is two kinds of apparel. Many's the time I have hit the lower Brule dressed like an Eskimo, and then gone upstream and cooled my feet by dangling them over the side of a canoe.

A good many of the faithful, like the President of the Old Duck Hunters' Association, Inc., are firm believers in celebrating the opening along the more arctic portions of the Brule. There is sound reason for this. At the average opening many of the big, migratory rainbows from Lake Superior have finished spawning and are working back to the home waters.

"A man would be a ninnyhammer," said Mister President to me, "to pass up that first crack at the big ones."

"Habit is a powerful thing," said I.

Well did he know my affection for the upper reaches and its chance for trout, albeit smaller ones, on smaller lures: namely and to wit, dry floating flies, than which no finer device to deceive fish has been conceived in the mind of man.

Anyway, we went fishing on the lower river, come opening day. It was a morning to gladden pneumonia specialists. Emerging from the warm car at the streamside, I was as eager to embrace the flood as I am to get up in a deer camp and light the fire. Braver men than I have quailed at such fishing. I can remember huge Carl Tarsrud, stellar Brule fisherman, six feet four of Viking stamina, declaring in John Ziegler's gun repair shop that he wouldn't have any part of that lower Brule on an ugly first day.

Well, there we were, us Old Duck Hunters, as far asunder in fraternal spirit as ever we were. It made me shiver just to look at that part of the Brule. We were down below Armstead's farm, north of the town of Brule. There were snowy patches in the hollows, the day was gray, and from the lake blew a searching cold.

The Rt. Hon. President was lively as a cricket. His brown eyes snapped. He had buckled into waders while I was pulling on extra socks—reluctantly. For him the birds were singing and the sun was shining. In him the flame of the zealot burns with a fierce light. He went to the river whistling. I followed in a dampened frame of mind.

Against the rigors of the day I had seen to it that there was a full quart thermos of scalding coffee in my jacket. I knew, too, that the President was similarly fortified, from the bulge in his own jacket. As I waded out into the rocky stream it came to me that, if worst came to worst, it was always possible to go ashore, light a fire, and drown my woes guzzling coffee.

Hizzoner had no thought of coffee at the moment. He hastened away down the little path on the left bank and embraced the current a hundred yards below me. This was duck soup for him. You knew, watching even at that distance, no shiver passed through his wiry frame, and you thought, disgusted, what frightful fanaticism possesses a man who thus cleaves to his private poison

*Fishing postcard humor, circa 1940.*

under any conditions.

I remember how cold I got. I remember how my hands got blue, how I dreaded changing flies or plucking with numb fingers for lethargic angleworms in the bait can. I remember how the river cold bit through waders and wool and drove me, time and again, to perching on stream rocks. I remember how I thought wader pockets would be handy things to have, and how I pressed hands into armpits to restore warmth.

But, best of all, I remember the big splash I made when worn hobnails betrayed me and I bounced, more horizontal than vertical, off a flat rock into four feet of water. Then the river claimed me completely, so that my under wools and my outer wools were soaked and only a wild grab saved my hat from drifting away.

Ah—the coffee! And the warming fire! A big one. And may the devil fly away with every rainbow trout in the lower Brule, for all of me. They weren't hitting anyway. Blessed coffee. Blessed fire.

Now for a match. Whazzat, no match-safe? Had I left it home this evil day, after toting it for years and years? I had, verily. Oh, foolish man. Oh, bitter cold. Well, the coffee, then. And quick, Henri, for there's a man freezing to death! Ah—a whole quart, scalding hot!

I unscrewed the aluminum top and gazed into a container in which the fragile glass shell had broken into a million pieces. Those old, smooth hobs on my wading brogues had not only half drowned me, but had delivered the thermos to mine enemy, the rock.

A pretty pickle. In ten minutes I'd be ready for an oxygen tent. I have fallen into many a river and many a lake. Annually I achieve swan dives, jack-knifes, half-gainers and standing-sitting-standing performances. I am an expert faller-in. Poling a canoe up Big Falls on the Brule, I can, any day you name, describe a neat parabola and come up dripping with only one shin skinned. On my better days I can weave back and forth in exaggerated slow motion until the waters finally claim me.

*A fly fisherman searches for trout lurking in the lee of an arched stone bridge. (Photograph © Dale C. Spartas/The Green Agency)*

Be assured, gentlemen, you are listening to no raw beginner at the diving game. But that one down below Armstead's farm really won me the championship of the Brule that season. That one was an even more convincing demonstration than one of several years before, when I fell head first out of a duck boat and went home by the light of the moon, strictly naked, my underwear drying on an oar.

"For two bits," I said, thinking of Mister President, "I would go look him up and give him a taste of it himself." It was just then the trail bushes parted, and there he was, dry as a bone, grinning like a skunk eating bumblebees, the tail of a big rainbow projecting from his game pocket. He took me in at a glance.

"Fell in on purpose so I'd feel sorry for you and we'd go to the upper river, eh?"

So much for sympathy from this Spartan who, when he falls in, keeps right on a-going. Nevertheless he produced his hot coffee and dry matches. While the fire roared and I draped clothing on bushes, he told me about the fish. "Down by those old pilings. Salmon eggs. I went downstream with him forty yards. He was in the air half the time."

Then he noticed that his ghillie was, in fact, in the blue-lipped stage. He took off his jacket, threw it around me and pushed me closer to the fire, throwing down birch bark for me to stand upon. It seemed to me there lurked in his eyes a twinkle of sympathy, but I can never make sure about that with him. It may be deviltry. He built a drying frame for the wet clothes, and when an hour had passed and I was back into them, half dry and very smoky, he relented completely. He went the whole hog.

"Well, come on. You'll never get completely dry down here. I've got my kitchen-sink fish anyway."

The President thus describes the whale which he must annually stretch out in the sink before calling in the neighbors.

So it was that we pulled out of the lower Brule valley and drove south. In the town of Brule he stopped the car and went into a store with his now empty thermos bottle.

"A man has got to have coffee to fish," he said.

It was only around noon, and this far up the Brule valley the sun was shining. South we went over familiar trails: the ranger's road past round-as-a-dime Hooligan Lake, the county trunk, past Winnebojou where three hundred cars were parked and thence to Stone's Bridge where Johnny Degerman presided. Up there it was 75 above. There was a strong, gusty wind beating. It was summer, and a few minutes before we had been in winter.

Let it be said here that on opening day along the Brule people who like to be alone will do best to stay above Winnebojou. Along this portion of the creek, for some twenty miles, most of the banks are owned privately, and ingress to same is not to be had at every turn-in gate along the county roads that parallel the stream. But the problem can be solved by going to Stone's Bridge, the common jumping-off place for upper river explorers.

If it is feasible to divide any river into two parts, the division may be effected on the Brule by nominating the Winnebojou Bridge as the equator. And connoisseurs of the difference between fact and fancy should be told, right here and now, that people who really know the creek will always refer to this particular spot as the Winnebojou Wagon Bridge, and you can figure out yourself when the last wagon crossed any bridge anywhere.

Still that is its traditional name. Upstream from it lie several million dollars' worth of real estate and lodges, including the fabulous Pierce estate of 4,400 acres. Downstream from it are the precincts of Tom, Dick and Harry and, let it be added, the best places for getting the big rainbows in the early run.

It was so warm up there at Stone's Bridge that Johnny Degerman, Charon of these waters, had his shirt open all the way down the front.

"Mr. Degerman, I believe," said the President in his best manner.

"Go to hell, the both of you," said Mr. Degerman, who was being bothered some by mosquitoes.

"Mr. Degerman!" the President reprimanded.

"I saved a canoe," said Johnny. "Thought you might be along. Could have rented it for five bucks. And all I get from you birds is a buck."

"Mr. Degerman," said the President, "your philanthropy moves me to the extent of promising to pay one buck and a half for said canoe."

"Lucky if I get the buck," said Johnny, who is a charming fellow. "And say, if you're smart, you'll show

*The romance of fly fishing lies as much in the beauty of a mountain stream, a perfect cast, and the ultimate catch as it does in the art of trout and salmon fishing equipment. The reel in the center of this photograph was manufactured around 1910 by the famous A. F. Meisselbach & Bro. company of Newark, New Jersey, during the golden age of machine-made American fishing reels. The Horricks-Ibbotson rod was handmade about 1920. Memorabilia owner: Pete Press. (Photograph © Howard Lambert)*

them something wet and big and brown. Carl Miller has been knocking their ears off with a big home-made Ginger Quill."

"Enough!" cried Hizzoner. "First you insult me, and then you rub it in by telling me what to throw at 'em. Gimme a canoe pole. I mean give him one. My back ain't so strong today."

So it was that the old Duck Hunters went forth abroad upon the bosom of the Brule and Mr. Degerman called after us, "I may pick up some chubs for you off'n the bridge, in case you don't connect."

We were too far away for the President to do more than look back at Johnny with what must pass as a haughty stare.

It was certainly a day. There was that downstream breeze, which means warmth. There was the smell of a million cedar trees. There was a good canoe under us, and ten miles of red-hot river before us, and hundreds and hundreds of cedar waxwings letting on they were glad to be alive.

You know how it is. The signs are right. You feel history is in the making. You take your time buttering up the line. You are painstaking about soaping the surplus grease off the leader. You lay on the anti-mosquito kalsomine. You light a leisurely pipe and don't give a rap what happens tomorrow or the day after.

His nibs exercised seniority rights by occupying the bow with a rod the first hour. It was not too eventful. Small trout could be had for the casting, willing wallopers, mostly rainbows and brookies, which fought with terrier impudence. The worthier foes were lurking under the banks and in the deep holes. The only memorable excitement in five miles was a dusky native of about 16 inches which came out from under a brush heap to take the President's wet Cowdung.

For long years those upper Brule brookies have intrigued the O.D.H.A., Inc. We do not credit them with too much sense. But accuse us not of sacrilege, for we love them dearly. We love them so much that we wish they had more—well, foresight. In a hitting mood they are fly-rushers, show-offs, and that is the trouble. More common caution and less eagerness to lick the world would save many of them useless flops in the bottom of a willow-walled hereafter.

"Did I ever tell you about the Olson boys?" said the President at lunch at May's Rips. "They were tak-

ing out pine on a forty near Foxboro, and it was a whale of a big forty, because they got about a million feet off it one winter.

"Anyway, one morning, the kid—I forget his name—woke up late in the camp and began dressing. He couldn't find his socks, which is what happens to anyone who wakes up late in a well-regulated logging camp. So he says, says he: "Some low-down, no-good miscreant without the decency of a weasel swiped my socks! Was it you, Pa?"

There was more. Of Jack Bradley's aniline-dyed pigeons which he sold to visiting trout fishermen on the Big Balsam in the old days as holy birds of India. Of the same Jack's famous kangaroo court, where fishermen were sentenced for ungraceful lying. Of times along the storied Brule when lumberjacks took out brook trout by the bushel on red-flannel-baited hooks. And there were tales of Old Mountain, the Brule's mythical gargantua, a rainbow trout whose ascent of the stream raised the water two feet; of his sworn enemy, the Mule, another rainbow, almost as big. That sort of thing didn't catch many fish, but along the Brule you are likely to feel it doesn't make any difference, one way or another.

We sat there, with our backs against cool cedars, and watched the river hustle by. Sometimes a canoe drifted past and a lazy hand would be raised, or a lazier Chippewa would exert himself for a minute, poling up the not-too-formidable fast water of May's Rips. But mostly we just sat and studied foam-flecked water spill down the rips, arrow into a water spear-head at the bottom and carom off to the left. It was almost three o'clock when the President leaped up.

"I don't know why in time I go fishing with you," he declared. "The day is almost over, and I've got only one kitchen-sink fish."

"Gimme," said I, "another doughnut—and shut up, will you?"

But the spell was broken. Mister President was on his feet and there was a river to fish. I took the stern paddle, for it was my turn, and the canoe slid down May's Rips under the rustic bridge, past the Pierce hatchery outflow through the wide-spread and down threatening Big Falls, which looks worse than it is, but is bad enough.

Big Falls is just a good fast rip of river, almost com-

*A gentleman angler hauls in another fine catch in this 1950s postcard scene.*

pletely arched by graceful cedars. You see it from the upstream side as hardly more than an inviting dark tunnel in the cedar forest wall. You see a little lip of curling water; and then when you are right on top of it and your eyes are adjusted to its darker light, you see it as a downhill stretch of roaring water, and unless you are good at twisting canoes around right-angled corners you may have trouble at the end, where it goes off to the left.

Big Falls is just another rapid to a good Brule Chippewa boatman. But neither the President nor I qualify in that respect. We are fair, just fair. On good days, when we are not too tired, we can, with care, bring a canoe back up Big Falls, a stunt the Chippewas do with a passenger—usually sitting, tensed, in the bottom. Well, Big Falls has licked me more often than vice versa, but I am resigned to winning up to about the eighth round, after which I fall in, or out, and grab the bow of the canoe and tow it the rest of the way.

We got down easily, and in the slack water the President said: "Hold 'er! Hold 'er and give me my waders."

For once, I had thought, we were to hit the upper river without recourse to long halts while Mister President climbed in and out of waders. It was not to be so, however. He had his same old scheme in mind: to tie up the canoe and wade the fast water below the Big Falls. He is a man who holds that the best way to catch trout is to meet them on their own terms, afoot.

Below Big Falls the Brule is touch-and-go wading in many spots. It goes down and it twists. It shoots between banks of huge gray cedars, and in places the trees almost meet overhead. Its bottom is rock-strewn. Its current is swift. Here, you would say, is a hunk of river that would be at home in the mountains.

Big fish have come out of that water. Springs seep out of the banks, and watercress flourishes in the sodden places where the river and terra firma contest for control. All of it—river, bank and trees—are forest

*"The desire for fishing is like some diseases, in attacking a man with great severity without notice. It can be no more resisted than falling in love can be resisted, and, like love, the best treatment is its gratification." —Charles Bradford, "Trout Truths" (Photograph © Richard Hamilton Smith)*

sponge, and through this rolls gin-white water over knobby bottoms.

I saw Hizzoner get down to business with salmon eggs and spinner. I went at it myself with Degerman's recommended Ginger Quill. Oh, there were fish. There are always frying-pan fish in this stretch. Mostly rainbows, here and there a brown that forgot to wait until night, and some brooks. In such swift water things can be very exciting with nothing more than a foot of fish on a line.

I saw the good fish—the No. 2 kitchen-sink fish—hit. It was Mister President's salmon eggs he coveted. A rainbow tardy in its return from waters so far upstream. But there was nothing tardy about the way it whacked the salmon eggs. These fish conjure up a kind of electrical insanity when they feel cold steel.

Hizzoner gave it the butt and yelled. I climbed out on the bank and went down there to view the quarrel. It was getting on toward evening. The river chill was rising.

Mister President's rod—the one with the long cork grip to ease the hand—got a workout that day. Above the rapids he yelled, "For the love of—"

The rest of his conversation was swallowed by river sounds, for it is so noisy in those rips that you can smile at a partner, call him a no-good stiff and he will actually think you are complimenting him. However, I gathered that the President desired that I make a pass at the big rainbow with a little metal-rimmed net which I carried. His own deep-bellied net was back in the canoe.

The fish was a good, standard, spring-run Brule job. Maybe around five pounds. Six pounds, possibly. My net was no instrument for him, but that's what I thought Hizzoner had ordered, and I went to work, all eyes on the fish.

He let him leap, up and down and across. There is no stopping these fellows when they start. Not for nothing do they wear that red badge of courage along the lateral line. When they act tired of plowing the top water, they just lie like stubborn terriers holding to a kid's skipping rope and tug-jerk! jerk! jerk!

Mister President was bellowing over the roar of water. I did not hear him. I was intent on getting that little net under the fish. The rainbow was brought close. I saw him a few feet from me—a hard, swift bullet of a fish, ready for another dash.

My time had come, and I swooped. I swooped with the net and missed.

Only in nightmares do I recall it clearly. The rim of the net touched that walloper somewhere, and with one powerful twist he was off and away, a shadowy torpedo heading for deep water.

I was a bit downstream from his nibs. I worked back toward him so that I could hear what he had been shouting. Coming closer, I heard: "I was telling you all the time to go back to the canoe and get my net, dern ye!"

That must have unnerved me, for when I got near him a foot slipped. I reached out for support, got hold of Mister President's shoulder and both of us went down.

To this day the Hon. President refers to that stretch as "the place where I swam the Brule, and later hanged a man on a handy cedar tree."

It was too late for a drying fire. There were miles of upstream poling ahead of us. We had the Big Falls to negotiate the hard way. So we got in the canoe and started. Mister President took the rear; I worked a shorter pole in the bow.

Half-way up, I knew we'd make it. We synchronized well as a poling team. The old knack was there. We would both heave with the poles at just the right instant, and get a fresh hold on the bottom at the right time. For once, said I, the Big Falls would find me triumphant.

Only one of us made it, and it was not I. With about ten feet more to go, the canoe gave a sudden and unaccountable jerk, not caused by rocks, you understand. Once more yours truly was overboard. That one, as I recall, was a quick back dive, and while I floundered, waist deep, Hizzoner shot the canoe up the last curling lip of the rapids.

To this day he will admit nothing. He declares such occurrences are part of the hazards of the game. He avers maybe his pole did slip a bit when it should have remained firm, that maybe he did shift his feet just a trifle. But as for admitting he put me overboard—"You know I wouldn't do a thing like that."

It was getting dark when I caught up with him at the head of Big Falls. He was grinning and had his recently filled thermos bottle open and ready for me. I

*Currier & Ives lithograph of a hooked trout, circa 1880.*

wrung out such garments as I could and thanked the stars for that warm coffee. I raised it to my lips there in the dusk, and I was chilled to the core.

It contained only ice-water. Ice-water! Of which I had recently drunk enough to float the canoe. From the semi-darkness came his voice: "I thought you'd get so hot up here on the upper river you'd need a cooling drink."

Later, while warming with the upstream poling job, he said that once he saved a man's life. The man had fallen in a lake and was well-nigh a goner. He fished the fellow out, squeezed out the water and restored him to consciousness with a hatful of lake water dashed into his face. The fellow came around, said Mister President, ran his tongue over his lips where the water lingered and said, "Dang it, you know I never tech the stuff!"

So we went home with only one kitchen-sink fish, and I was warm as toast long before we got to Johnny Degerman's dock. Which may have been from exertion with a canoe pole, or may have been from listening to the President of the Old Duck Hunters' Association, Inc.

## Fishing Equipment Goes to War

When the United States entered World War II, companies that in peacetime made rods, reels, and other fishing equipment were called upon to support the war effort.

The fact that they were not manufacturing fishing equipment did not deter these companies from advertising their products during the war years, however. Instead of cutting back their advertising efforts, these companies adjusted their ads to appeal to America's swelling patriotism. Many of the fishing equipment ads during wartime congratulated the company's own role in the war effort, while other ads promoted the fact that the company's products were being used by American soldiers.

Here are just a few examples of advertisements featured by fishing equipment manufacturers during World War II. The companies' patriotism can be seen in their references to "our boys" and victory, in the taglines encouraging consumers to buy war bonds and conserve resources, and in the Army-Navy flag graphics included in many of the ads.

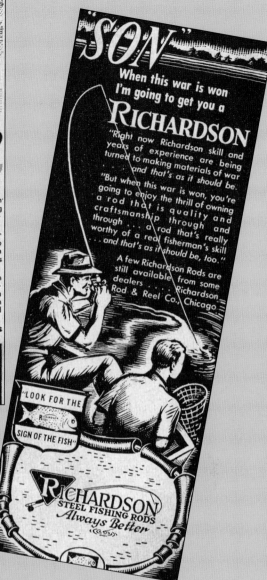

# SUMMERTIME, AND THE LIVIN' WAS EASY

## By Robert Ruark

Robert Chester Ruark (1915–1965) is probably the most loved of all hunting writers. Like Ernest Hemingway, Ruark was a journalist as well as a best-selling author; his novels include *Something of Value* (1955) and *Poor No More* (1959). But hunters remember him best for his well-crafted pieces that began appearing in *Field & Stream* in the early 1950s.

In 1952, the magazine inaugurated Ruark's column "The Old Man and the Boy," which told the story of a remarkable friendship between a boy and his grandfather. Together, the duo hunt the woods of North Carolina, and fish the lakes and sea. The Old Man serves as both teacher and guide, passing on his hunting and fishing lore—as well as his wisdom. The boy was an autobiographical portrait of Ruark; in an author's note, he writes, "Anybody who reads this book is bound to realize that I had a real fine time as a kid."

The column was collected into book form under the same title and originally published in 1957, earning a place on the bookshelves of several generations of hunters and anglers. This excerpt from *The Old Man and the Boy* tells the story of a fishing trip—but along the way it also delves deeper into the relationship between man and boy, and people and fishing, illuminating timeless truths with poignancy and eloquence.

*A grandfather teaches his young grandson the secrets to the perfect cast. (Photograph © Alan and Sandy Carey)*

JUNE IS A nice time of year, because school lets out and it hasn't got real hot yet. The mornings are fresh and dewy and everything is green and sweet-smelling, and generally the mosquitoes haven't started and the nights are still cool enough for covers. The nicest thing about June is that the awful memories of school are behind you, and September is so far away that it doesn't even count. The summertime belongs to boys. Grown-up folks might play around at the beaches and the country clubs and take vacations, but summer truly belongs to kids. It's sunburn time and ground-itch time and poison-ivy time. It's barefoot time and fishhooks-caught-in-your-ear time and baseball time and whip-poorwill time and bullbats-swooping-low-in-the-dusk time.

Seems to me the summertime had so much good stuff in it that it should have been made illegal for most people. You had all sorts of wonderful things to give you the bellyache—peaches and pears and wild berries and tame berries, such as raspberries and strawberries, and the big purple plums and the yellow-and-rose plums, and the figs, and the big cool green watermelons or the tiger-striped ones that you took out of the cold water in the springhouse and ate by just shoving your face in and chewing on through. Finally, as the summer would wear on and it began to smell a little smoky in the air, like fall was knocking, the grapes came—the big, fat, juice-bursting scuppernongs, white and chokingly sweet, and the slightly tart black ones, as big as golf balls.

In my town they closed up Sunday school as well as regular school in June, which suited me just fine. About all I ever learned in Sunday school was how to shoot craps down in the basement, a pastime so deplorable that Mr. James Stebbins, the sandy-haired Englishman (a foreigner!) who tried to domesticate us young demons, eventually renovated our shocking morals by ringing in a pair of loaded dice and busting us all for the spring term of religious worship. He was as steely as a professional bookmaker about the IOU's, and he put all his ill-got gains into the collection plate. I remember I was just paid out, and was feeling pretty religious about it, when the Old Man cornered me one morning after breakfast.

It was one of those days when a boy figures he's got to pop if something doesn't happen to him—some-thing big, something adventurous, something stupendous, like saving a maiden fair from the wild animals that have busted loose from the circus, or rushing into a burning building to rescue a child, or something. Anything. Making tar balls out of the bubbling asphalt pavement wasn't enough. Eating plums that were too green or trying out a sneaky slingshot on a catbird wasn't enough. It was one of those days you maybe remember, with the bobolinks balanced on the bending grasses in the breeze, and the Baltimore orioles scattering notes around like millionaires throwing coins, and the wild cherries black and sweating sweet on the big leafy tree with the Tarzan house built into it.

The Old Man stabbed me with his pipe stem and his eyes. "I been hearing about you," he said. "I been hearing a lot of things about you—about how you cut Sunday school every other Sunday, and about that dice game you young hellions started down in the basement at Saint James', and it seems to me you are doomed for perdition. I thought I had you straightened out in the school business, but now I reckon I got to teach you a little humility."

Here she comes, I said to myself. I'm goin' to get preached at, or made to do something I don't want to without knowing why I don't want to. The Old Man was awful shifty when he come down hard with the parables according to Himself.

"What are you goin' to do?" I asked him.

"Fishin'," he said cheerfully. "We're just goin' fishin'."

Now, you certainly don't punish a boy for irreverence by taking him fishing; so there has got to be a catch in this one somewhere, I thought. But I had learned from the Old Man to play pretty cosy; so all I said was, "What kind of fishin'?"

"Fresh-water," the Old Man said. "Maybe catch us a big ol' bass or so, or at least a mess of brim. We'll take the Liz and rent us a boat from a man I know on Big Crick. Wait till I go get the rods, and while I'm after them you go roll over some rotten logs and see if you can turn your undoubted talents to filling a tin can full of worms."

I ambled down to the cow lot, behind which there was a low, wet swamp where the pigs rooted and the quail came to drink, and turned over a few old punky logs and filled up a big paint can with fine fat worms,

*Northern pike and muskies, known as "freshwater barracuda," were always a test of anglers and their tackle. The tasty lure at the end of the musky rod is a giant eight-inch (20-cm) James Heddon and Sons Vamp, made from 1925 to 1929. The jointed-body lure with single hooks resting on the boat's transom is a Tarpalunge made by the Shakespeare Bait Company of Kalamazoo, Michigan. The pine-wood tacklebox by the Tronic Trunk Company had a water-tight gasket and was called the "Life Saving Box" as you could use it as a float if your fishing boat capsized. Memorabilia owner: Northland Fishing Museum of Osseo, Wisconsin. (Photograph © Howard Lambert)*

just as happy as worms to be wriggling around in the loose, wet dirt I put in the can. When I got back to the house, the Old Man had produced a couple of light split-bamboo rods and a couple of little reels that I never had seen before.

"Where'd they come from?" I asked the Old Man.

"Oh," he said, "I've had 'em around for a long time. There's a lot of things I got you don't know about. I ain't a man to take every whippersnapper I meet into my confidence. I got plenty of secrets I ain't talkin' about. These rods are one of my secrets. On this coast it's supposed to be sissy to fish fresh water—either sissy or downright po' barkerish." A po' barker is the kind of shiftless white trash who would be so trifling that he'd have to feed his family off perch and catfish.

I cranked the Liz, and we snorted off. I never went off in the old Liz without snickering a little bit. The Old Man said only a monkey was fit to drive one of the old T-models. "You need both hands on the wheel, both feet on the pedals, and a tail to keep the door shut," he said. But they never built a better car. It would go anywhere that one of those Army tanks would go, and with about the same amount of noise. It rode high off the ground and looked like an old lady with her skirts held up off the mud, but it never wore out.

We drove about fifteen miles and came up to Big Crick. It had some other name, I suppose, but Big Crick was what we called it. Actually, it was a little river that connected up somewhere with the Cape Fear River. There were a boathouse and a landing and a few skiffs pulled up alongside the landing. When we got there, it was about four o'clock in the afternoon.

The Old Man paid fifty cents for the rent of a boat. He just indicated the oars to me with a jerk of his head, and I started pulling upstream in the slow, brown, leaf-dyed waters, against a lazy current that made little ripples and bubbles and sucking sounds as it ran over and around little rocks and old green-lichened snags. While I rowed, the Old Man fussed with the fishing gear. I noticed that he put a split shot and a single hook on one leader, and tied a bright red-and-white wooden lure with some pork-rind streamers on the other.

*Luckily for Junior, Dad was riding by on his trusty John Deere when a feisty turtle snagged his hook at the old fishing hole, in this painting by artist Walter Haskell Hinton. (Artwork © Deere & Company)*

*An angler works the shoreline on a glorious summer day. (Photograph © Richard Hamilton Smith)*

*This largemouth bass seems determined to give the angler a run for his money. (Photograph © Doug Stamm/ProPhoto)*

We came around a bend of the Big Crick, and the Old Man told me to head her into the bank, where there were a lot of lily pads and weeds and, it looked like, some fairly deep pools. He handed me the rod with the single hook and the little sinker on it.

"Now," he said sternly, "we will fish. You will use some of those worms you dug up and catch us a mess of brim. I will see if I can't do something about a bass or so. When you've caught us a bait o' brim, switch the hook and try for the bass yourself. They won't be bitin' for another hour or so, anyhow, until the evening fly hatch rises.

"Now, then, son," the Old Man said, "we ain't goin' to talk any, because fishin' is a silent sport and a lot of conversation scares the fish and wrecks the mood. What I want you to do is set there and fish, and when the fish ain't bitin' I want you to listen and look and think. Think about heaven and hell and just how long is hereafter. Look around you and don't take nothing for granted. Look at everything you see and listen to everything you hear, just like you were brand-new come from another world, and think about all those things and how they got there. Now let's fish."

I threaded a big, juicy worm onto the hook and flipped the line over the side, and in less than a minute a big fat bream had seized onto it and I jerked him into the boat. They only ran about half a pound apiece, but they bit like they hadn't ever seen a worm and thought it was candy. The Old Man was potting away at lily pads or close aboard them and flicking his line along the shore under overhangs of old logs or rocks, and wasn't catching anything at all.

I pulled in about two dozen bream, and then switched to a plug and started to imitate the Old Man. I had a little trouble with the wrist, but not much, because I had been doing a lot of salt-water fishing, and I'd learned to throw a cast net, and boys don't have much trouble learning anything outside of book lessons. Nothing hit my hook either. It was just flip, reel in, poise, flip, and reel in some more, with the bait hitting the water with a *plonk* and the pork streamers making a wriggle in the water like a frog kicking his legs in a breast stroke.

Well, sir, when you can't talk, you got to think and look and listen, and all of a sudden I was the lonesomest boy in the world. You know anything about what it's like in a fresh-water swamp in the South when the sun is starting to drop and the noises begin? Or what it smells like and feels like as it cools off from the heat of the day? And what sort of things are all around you?

I got to looking at the water. It was clear and clean, but as brown as your hat from the leaf dye, and when you scooped up a handful it tasted a little like leaves smelled if you crumpled them in your hand. And it was full of all sorts of little things—bugs that hopped and popped, little crawlers that left a tiny wake behind them, like a mink swimming. Fish swirled and rose to snap at the first beginnings of the fly hatch. A big bullfrog gave a loud, croaking *ker-tunk!* and leaped into the water with a splash. Over on the other bank a water moccasin slithered down the greasy earth and slipped into the water without a sound.

It was so lonely in that swampy river that it made you want to cry. All the sad sounds in the world suddenly started. A dove set up that woeful *oo-hoo-oo-hoo-hoo* across the swamp, and another one, sadder still, began to answer him back. They sounded like two old widow women swapping miseries.

In the utter hush a million noises intruded. A bittern roared. A heron squawked. A kingfisher rattled. A deer snorted and barked. A bird screeched. A crow cawed. Somewhere deep in the swamp there was a growl and a scream as a wildcat skittled a rabbit. A squirrel chirred and was answered. Leaves rustled. Things fell off trees. Bushes stirred mysteriously with the passing of unseen animals. Along the creek a piece a raccoon came down to drink, washing his little paws as daintily as a lady.

The sun sank lower, and the huge old live oaks, their Spanish-moss beards swaying down to the water's edge, looked as ominous as monsters. The cypress knees made all sorts of strange shapes. Along the banks the ferns grew—the delicate maidenhair fern and broader-leafed ones I didn't know the names of—in an indescribable carpetry of cool greenness. Little silly flowers poked their button heads up among the ferns.

Away off somewhere a cowbell tinkled very sadly, and you could hear a rich Negro voice singing its way through the frightening, falling shadows of the intruding evening. He sounded scared, and he was scared, and he wouldn't get any less scared until he sighted his shack with the fire going under the big black iron kettle.

Now the cicadas and the crickets and all the other loudly vocal bugs were beginning to sound their eventide notes, like an orchestra tuning for the overture.

In my brain I looked at all of it—the trees, the grass, the moss, the bugs, the birds, the ferns, the flowers, the setting sun, the rising hatch of flies. I felt the dark creeping and saw the first shining speck of star and heard the mounting noises in the swamp. I felt cold in my bones from the rising miasma of mist as the air cooled. I was so lost in what was going on, in the million slivers of vibrant life, that when a big fish hit I lost him out of sheer panic.

The bass bit beautifully, there just at dusk, and we caught ten or so between us—not very big; but a two-pound bigmouth on a whippy rod is quite an order. When it got black-dark, the fish eased off and I shoved the boat into the stream and let the current carry us down toward the landing. The Old Man took in the lines and put the plugs back in the tackle box, and I just sort of warded the scow off the snags. The Old Man lit his pipe and puffed peacefully. He said nothing, nothing at all.

It was main late when we hit the landing. The stars had crept out bright now, and a little wedge of moon was slipping sneaky-like up over the trees. The frogs, the bugs, the night birds, and the animals were making a din. I got to thinking about eternity, and how long something that never ended would be, and I got to thinking about how much trouble Somebody went to, to make things like cocoons that butterflies come out of, and seasons and rain and moss on trees, and frogs and fish and possums and coons and quail and flowers and ferns and water and moons and suns and stars and winds. And boys. Especially boys.

Once we got back in the Liz, the Old Man didn't say anything for a few miles. Then he spoke, without turning his head. "You ain't said much. What do you feel like?"

"I feel like I been to church. I feel like I got—that word you said."

"Humility?" the Old Man asked gently.

"Yessir," I said. "I feel awful little and unimportant, somehow, and a little bit scared."

"You're beginning to learn, boy," he said. "You're beginning to learn."

## Those Fabulous Outboard Motors

The advent of the gasoline-powered outboard motor signaled a revolution in fishing. With a motor bolted to the back of their boat, anglers could now travel faster and farther to reach new fishing holes, and all of the armwork that had gone into rowing could now be used in casting.

Classic outboard motors have become highly collectible in recent years as anglers revive and polish these old works of mechanical art. These ads highlight several of the new-fangled motors from the early days.

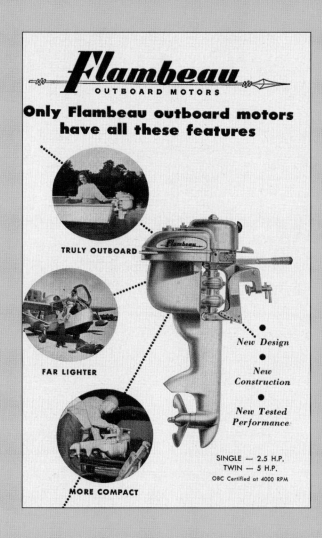

# THE HUNCHBACK TROUT

## By Richard Brautigan

In 1961, Richard Brautigan (1935–1984) left his beatnik life in San Francisco behind. He loaded up his family and all the camping gear he could gather, and aimed his veteran Plymouth station wagon at the Idaho wilderness. His back-to-the-land venture became the inspiration for his most famous novel, *Trout Fishing in America* (1967), which sold more than two million copies during the Summer of Love and became a surreal bible that helped define a generation of alienated hippies.

Brautigan went on to pen several other quintessentially '60s and '70s novels and collections of poems that found an almost cultlike audience, including *The Pill Versus the Springhill Mine Disaster* (1968), *A Confederate General from Big Sur* (1968), and *Rommel Drives on Deep into Egypt* (1970).

*Trout Fishing in America* only incidently concerns itself with fishing, but this chapter—while not offering any solid how-to angling advice or philosophical truths about the fishing life—well reflects the turmoil of the decade.

The creek was made narrow by little green trees that grew too close together. The creek was like 12,845 telephone booths in a row with high Victorian ceilings and all the doors taken off and all the backs of the booths knocked out.

Sometimes when I went fishing in there, I felt just like a telephone repairman, even though I did not look like one. I was only a kid covered with fishing tackle, but in some strange way by going in there and catching a few trout, I kept the telephones in service. I was an asset to society.

It was pleasant work, but at times it made me uneasy. It could grow dark in there instantly when there were some clouds in the sky and they worked their way onto the sun. Then you almost needed candles to fish by, and foxfire in your reflexes.

Once I was in there when it started raining. It was dark and hot and steamy. I was of course on overtime. I had that going in my favor. I caught seven trout in fifteen minutes.

The trout in those telephone booths were good fellows. There were a lot of young cutthroat trout six to nine inches long, perfect pan size for local calls. Sometimes there were a few fellows, eleven inches or so— for the long distance calls.

I've always liked cutthroat trout. They put up a good fight, running against the bottom and then broad jumping. Under their throats they fly the orange banner of Jack the Ripper.

Also in the creek were a few stubborn rainbow trout, seldom heard from, but there all the same, like certified public accountants. I'd catch one every once in a while. They were fat and chunky, almost as wide as they were long. I've heard those trout called "squire" trout.

It used to take me about an hour to hitchhike to that creek. There was a river nearby. The river wasn't much. The creek was where I punched in. Leaving my card above the clock, I'd punch out again when it was time to go home.

I remember the afternoon I caught the hunchback trout.

A farmer gave me a ride in a truck. He picked me up at a traffic signal beside a bean field and he never said a word to me.

His stopping and picking me up and driving me down the road was as automatic a thing to him as closing the barn door, nothing need be said about it, but still I was in motion traveling thirty-five miles an hour down the road, watching houses and groves of trees go by, watching chickens and mailboxes enter and pass through my vision.

Then I did not see any houses for a while. "This is where I get out," I said.

The farmer nodded his head. The truck stopped. "Thanks a lot," I said.

The farmer did not ruin his audition for the Metropolitan Opera by making a sound. He just nodded his head again. The truck started up. He was the original silent old farmer.

A little while later I was punching in at the creek. I put my card above the clock and went into that long tunnel of telephone booths.

I waded about seventy-three telephone booths in. I caught two trout in a little hole that was like a wagon wheel. It was one of my favorite holes, and always good for a trout or two.

I always like to think of that hole as a kind of pencil sharpener. I put my reflexes in and they came back out with a good point on them. Over a period of a couple of years, I must have caught fifty trout in that hole, though it was only as big as a wagon wheel.

I was fishing with salmon eggs and using a size 14 single egg hook on a pound and a quarter test tippet. The two trout lay in my creel covered entirely by green fems, ferns made gentle and fragile by the damp walls of telephone booths.

The next good place was forty-five telephone booths in. The place was at the end of a run of gravel, brown and slippery with algae. The run of gravel dropped off and disappeared at a little shelf where there were some white rocks.

One of the rocks was kind of strange. It was a flat white rock. Off by itself from the other rocks, it reminded me of a white cat I had seen in my childhood. The cat had fallen or been thrown off a high wooden sidewalk that went along the side of a hill in Tacoma, Washington. The cat was lying in a parking lot below.

The fall had not appreciably helped the thickness of the cat, and then a few people had parked their cars on the cat. Of course, that was a long time ago and the cars looked different from the way they look now.

*An angler reels in a fine rainbow trout on the Obey River of Tennessee. (Photograph © Byron Jorjorian)*

You hardly see those cars any more. They are the old cars. They have to get off the highway because they can't keep up.

That flat white rock off by itself from the other rocks reminded me of that dead cat come to lie there in the creek, among 12,845 telephone booths.

I threw out a salmon egg and let it drift down over that rock and WHAM! a good hit! and I had the fish on and it ran hard downstream, cutting at an angle and staying deep and really coming on hard, solid and uncompromising, and then the fish jumped and for a second I thought it was a frog. I'd never seen a fish like that before.

God-damn! What the hell!

The fish ran deep again and I could feel its life energy screaming back up the line to my hand. The line felt like sound. It was like an ambulance siren coming straight at me, red light flashing, and then going away again and then taking to the air and becoming an air raid siren.

The fish jumped a few more times and it still looked like a frog, but it didn't have any legs. Then the fish grew tired and sloppy, and I swung and splashed it up the surface of the creek and into my net.

The fish was a twelve-inch rainbow trout with a huge hump on its back. A hunchback trout. The first I'd ever seen. The hump was probably due to an injury that occurred when the trout was young. Maybe a horse stepped on it or a tree fell over in a stomm or its mother spawned where they were building a bridge.

There was a fine thing about that trout. I only wish I could have made a death mask of him. Not of his body though, but of his energy. I don't know if anyone would have understood his body. I put it in my creel.

Later in the afternoon when the telephone booths began to grow dark at the edges, I punched out of the creek and went home. I had that hunchback trout for dinner. Wrapped in cornmeal and fried in butter, its hump tasted sweet as the kisses of Esmeralda.

ABOVE: *Silhouetted by the brilliant mountain sun, a fly fisherman on the South Fork of Idaho's Boise River scoops up his catch in a net. (Photograph © William H. Mullins)*

RIGHT: *What better way to pass a crisp late-fall afternoon than in a tranquil stream in Whitewater State Park in Minnesota? (Photograph © Richard Hamilton Smith)*

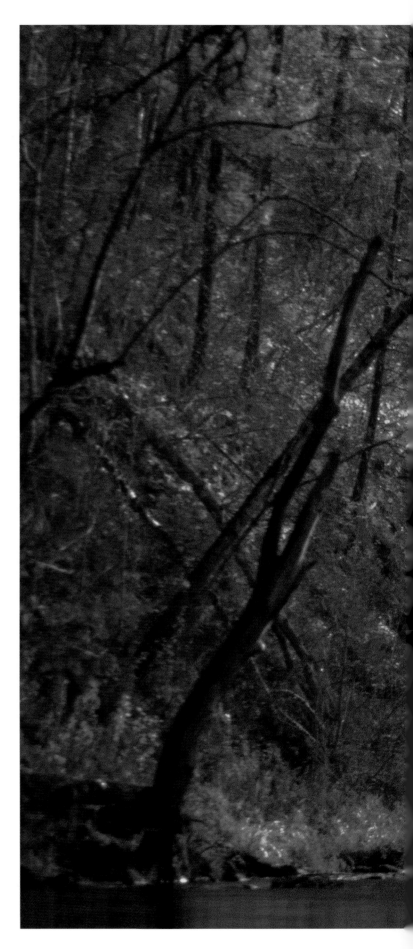

# A RIVER RUNS THROUGH IT

By Norman Maclean

**N**orman Maclean's novella, *A River Runs Through It,* contains perhaps the most famous of all fishing stories. It blends the esthetics of fly fishing with the glory of Montana and the poignant relationship between brothers to create a classic tale.

Maclean (1902–1990) was born in Iowa but grew up in Missoula, Montana, the land that courses through his stories. His father was a Presbyterian minister, and Maclean was a lifelong fly fisherman, lending this story autobiographical tones.

Maclean was a beloved professor at the University of Chicago, concentrating on teaching rather than creating a prolific body of work. His sole other book, *Young Men and Fire* (1992), published posthumously, took fourteen years of research and writing. In it, Maclean pays homage to thirteen young smokejumpers who perished in a dreadful forest fire at Mann Gulch, Montana, in 1949.

This excerpt from the beginning of the novella introduces many of Maclean's themes in a writing style that flows like a river under the summer sun.

*"As no man is born an artist, so no man is born an angler."* —*Izaak Walton,* The Compleat Angler
*(Photograph © Robert E. Barber)*

IN OUR FAMILY, there was no clear line between religion and fly fishing. We lived at the junction of great trout rivers in western Montana, and our father was a Presbyterian minister and a fly fisherman who tied his own flies and taught others. He told us about Christ's disciples being fishermen, and we were left to assume, as my brother and I did, that all first-class fishermen on the Sea of Galilee were fly fishermen and that John, the favorite, was a dry-fly fisherman.

It is true that one day a week was given over wholly to religion. On Sunday mornings my brother, Paul, and I went to Sunday school and then to "morning services" to hear our father preach and in the evenings to Christian Endeavor and afterwards to "evening services" to hear our father preach again. In between on Sunday afternoons we had to study *The Westminster Shorter Catechism* for an hour and then recite before we could walk the hills with him while he unwound between services. But he never asked us more than the first question in the catechism, "What is the chief end of man?" And we answered together so one of us could carry on if the other forgot, "Man's chief end is to glorify God, and to enjoy Him forever." This always seemed to satisfy him, as indeed such a beautiful answer should have, and besides he was anxious to be on the hills where he could restore his soul and be filled again to overflowing for the evening sermon. His chief way of recharging himself was to recite to us from the sermon that was coming, enriched here and there with selections from the most successful passages of his morning sermon.

Even so, in a typical week of our childhood Paul and I probably received as many hours of instruction in fly fishing as we did in all other spiritual matters.

After my brother and I became good fishermen, we realized that our father was not a great fly caster, but he was accurate and stylish and wore a glove on his casting hand. As he buttoned his glove in preparation to giving us a lesson, he would say, "It is an art that is performed on a four-count rhythm between ten and two o'clock."

As a Scot and a Presbyterian, my father believed that man by nature was a mess and had fallen from an original state of grace. Somehow, I early developed the notion that he had done this by falling from a tree. As for my father, I never knew whether he believed God

was a mathematician but he certainly believed God could count and that only by picking up God's rhythms were we able to regain power and beauty. Unlike many Presbyterians, he often used the word "beautiful."

After he buttoned his glove, he would hold his rod straight out in front of him, where it trembled with the beating of his heart. Although it was eight and a half feet long, it weighed only four and a half ounces. It was made of split bamboo cane from the far-off Bay of Tonkin. It was wrapped with red and blue silk thread, and the wrappings were carefully spaced to make the delicate rod powerful but not so stiff it could not tremble.

Always it was to be called a rod. If someone called it a pole, my father looked at him as a sergeant in the United States Marines would look at a recruit who had just called a rifle a gun.

My brother and I would have preferred to start learning how to fish by going out and catching a few, omitting entirely anything difficult or technical in the way of preparation that would take away from the fun. But it wasn't by way of fun that we were introduced to our father's art. If our father had had his say, nobody who did not know how to fish would be allowed to disgrace a fish by catching him. So you too will have to approach the art Marine- and Presbyterian-style, and, if you have never picked up a fly rod before, you will soon find it factually and theologically true that man by nature is a damn mess. The four-and-a-half-ounce thing in silk wrappings that trembles with the underskirt motions of the flesh becomes a stick without brains, refusing anything simple that is wanted of it. All that a rod has to do is lift the line, the leader, and the fly off the water, give them a good toss over the head, and then shoot them forward so they will land in the water without a splash in the following order: fly, transparent leader, and then the line—otherwise the fish will see the fly is a fake and be gone. Of course, there are special casts that anyone could predict would be difficult, and they require artistry—casts where the line can't go over the fisherman's head because cliffs or trees are immediately behind, sideways casts to get the fly under overhanging willows, and so on. But what's remarkable about just a straight cast—just picking up a rod with line on it and tossing the line across the river?

Well, until man is redeemed he will always take a

*The art of fly fishing is exemplified in this fly fisherman's collection of tackle. The tackle shown here includes a Pflueger Golden West reel in mint condition. It is mounted on a South Bend Cross Custom Built rod, Model 166. Memorabilia owner: Pete Press.*
*(Photograph © Howard Lambert)*

*The storm has passed and a rainbow takes its place. A group of anglers can now resume their work in the Yellowstone River of Oregon.*
*(Photograph © Dennis Frates)*

fly rod too far back, just as natural man always over-swings with an ax or golf club and loses all his power somewhere in the air; only with a rod it's worse, be-cause the fly often comes so far back it gets caught behind in a bush or rock. When my father said it was an art that ended at two o'clock, he often added, "closer to twelve than to two," meaning that the rod should be taken back only slightly farther than overhead (straight overhead being twelve o'clock).

Then, since it is natural for man to try to attain power without recovering grace, he whips the line back and forth making it whistle each way, and sometimes even snapping off the fly from the leader, but the power that was going to transport the little fly across the river somehow gets diverted into building a bird's nest of line, leader, and fly that falls out of the air into the water about ten feet in front of the fisherman. If, though, he pictures the round trip of the line, transparent leader, and fly from the time they leave the water until their return, they are easier to cast. They naturally come off the water heavy line first and in front, and light trans-parent leader and fly trailing behind. But, as they pass overhead, they have to have a little beat of time so the light, transparent leader and fly can catch up to the heavy line now starting forward and again fall behind it; otherwise, the line starting on its return trip will collide with the leader and fly still on their way up, and the mess will be the bird's nest that splashes into the water ten feet in front of the fisherman.

Almost the moment, however, that the forward order of line, leader, and fly is reestablished, it has to be reversed because the fly and transparent leader must be ahead of the heavy line when they settle on the water. If what the fish sees is highly visible line, what the fisherman will see are departing black darts, and he might as well start for the next hole. High overhead, then, on the forward cast (at about ten o'clock) the fisherman checks again.

The four-count rhythm, of course, is functional. The one count takes the line, leader, and fly off the water; the two count tosses them seemingly straight into the sky; the three count was my father's way of saying that at the top the leader and fly have to be given a little beat of time to get behind the line as it is starting forward; the four count means put on the power and throw the line into the rod until you reach ten

ABOVE: *It may be too dark to cast flies, but it's not too dark to tie them. And it's not too late to tell a tale or two of "the one that got away." (Photograph © Bill Buckley/The Green Agency)*

FACING PAGE: *An angler attempts to entrance and entice the trout in a Montana stream. (Photograph © Jim Noelker/The Green Agency)*

o'clock—then check-cast, let the fly and leader get ahead of the line, and coast to a soft and perfect landing. Power comes not from power everywhere, but from knowing where to put it on. "Remember," as my father kept saying, "it is an art that is performed on a four-count rhythm between ten and two o'clock."

My father was very sure about certain matters pertaining to the universe. To him, all good things—trout as well as eternal salvation—come by grace and grace comes by art and art does not come easy.

So my brother and I learned to cast Presbyterian-style, on a metronome. It was mother's metronome, which father had taken from the top of the piano in town. She would occasionally peer down to the dock from the front porch of the cabin, wondering nervously whether her metronome could float if it had to. When she became so overwrought that she thumped down the dock to reclaim it, my father would clap out the four-count rhythm with his cupped hands.

Eventually, he introduced us to literature on the subject. He tried always to say something stylish as he buttoned the glove on his casting hand. "Izaak Walton," he told us when my brother was thirteen or fourteen, "is not a respectable writer. He was an Episcopalian and a bait fisherman." Although Paul was three years younger than I was, he was already far ahead of me in anything relating to fishing and it was he who first found a copy of *The Compleat Angler* and reported back to me, "The bastard doesn't even know how to spell 'complete.' Besides, he has songs to sing to dairymaids." I borrowed his copy, and reported back to him, "Some of those songs are pretty good." He said, "Whoever saw a dairymaid on the Big Blackfoot River?

"I would like," he said, "to get him for a day's fishing on the Big Blackfoot—with a bet on the side."

The boy was very angry, and there has never been a doubt in my mind that the boy would have taken the Episcopalian.

# GRANDPA AND GRANDSON

By Red Smith

Walter Wellesley "Red" Smith (1905–1982) was one of the greatest sports journalists of all time. During his years at the Philadelphia *Record* and, subsequently, the New York *Herald Tribune*, he developed a keen knowledge of the sports world, a sharp eye for the human angle, and renown for his humor and command of the English language. His prowess as a reporter and columnist was recognized with the Pulitzer Prize in 1976.

Several collections of Smith's columns have appeared over the years, including *Out of the Red* (1950), *Red Smith on Fishing Around the World* (1963), *Strawberries in the Wintertime* (1974), *To Absent Friends from Red Smith* (1982), and *The Red Smith Reader* (1982). In addition, he edited a variety of anthologies of great sporting stories, among them *Sports Stories* (1949) and *Press Box: Red Smith's Favorite Sports Stories* (1993).

This column from the New York *Herald Tribune* touches on the ages-old relationship between grandfather and grandson and a classic fishing trip.

*A three-year-old fledgling enthusiast shows off his first rainbow trout. (Photograph © Ron Spomer)*

"Grandpa," the fisherman asked, watching his companion crawl under a barbed-wire fence, "did you grow old or were you made old?"

The fisherman had a little plastic rod and a spinning reel with a bobber on the line. He had dug worms out of a compost heap and now he dunked one in Turtle Pond on Ozzie Fischer's farm near Beetlebung Corner here on Martha's Vineyard. He watched the bobber intently, moving his bait here and there beside lily pads. White water lilies rested on the surface, their petals opened fully. Water striders darted about in cheeky defiance of natural laws. The fisherman noticed a wooden structure floating in the middle of the pond. "The dog has to swim to his house," he said. "It does look like a doghouse," he was told, "but Mr. Fischer built that for ducks in case they wanted to make a nest in it and lay their eggs."

Not even a turtle showed interest in the worm. This may explain why you never see anybody fishing Turtle Pond. However, the swan pond in West Tisbury was only a fifteen-minute drive down island and it is common to see boys fishing there. Probably the proper name is Mill Pond, but in the fisherman's family it is known as the swan pond because a cob and his pen live and love and rear their cygnets there. The couple's only child this year is already half the size of the parents.

The fisherman was thoughtful on the drive. "Do people who don't have a birthday grow older?" he asked.

Yes, he was told, there is one way to avoid that but the method isn't recommended.

"Some people don't have a birthday," he said. "They have to pick July." After a silence he added an afterthought. "Or December. I'd pick July."

"It's August now," he was reminded.

"Yes, but there'll be another July."

"Oh, you mean next July. Yes, there are always two—last July and next July." He thought that over and smiled as if the idea pleased him, but he made no comment.

The swans were at the far end of their pond. On the water beside the road were a dozen or more mallards. Parking, the fisherman's companion asked: "How old are you now?"

At first there was no answer. Then, tentatively: "Six."

"Oh? When will you be six?"

"Tomorrow." His birthday is in September.

Reddish-brown weeds showed a little below the surface. "Throw it where the ducks are," the fisherman said. He laughed when the bobber, split shot, and hook plopped in near a duck, startling her. "Now hold the rod still and watch the bobber," he was told.

"What's a bobber?"

"That red and white thing."

"That's a floater," he said, but not impatiently.

Drawn by curiosity, two ducks swam slowly toward the bobber, eyeing it.

"I have to go to the bathroom," the fisherman said. He saw some tall shrubs. "I'll go behind there." He went off at a trot.

While he was gone the bobber submerged, but the bait was lifted clear before a fish could strip the hook or, worse, get himself caught in the fisherman's absence.

"A fish pulled the floater underwater," he was told on his return. "Be ready to catch him."

In a few moments the bobber broke into a jig. The fisherman cranked his little tin reel. Except for a tiny nubbin of worm, the hook was bare.

"The worms are in the car," his companion said. "Keep fishing with that and I'll get another." By the time he got back the hook was clean.

"Next time the floater sinks," it was suggested, "jerk your rod up first to set the hook in the fish and then crank." In a moment: "There! Good, now crank. No, I'm afraid you're caught in the weeds. Just keep cranking. No! You have a fish. Keep cranking. See him?"

A pale belly flashed right, left and right again. His lips set, the fisherman reeled furiously. He dragged a nine-inch bullhead onto the bank and stared at it.

"Is that the first fish you ever caught?"

"Yes." The tone was hushed.

"Come on, then. We'll take it home and then I'll skin it so your mother can cook it."

"My mommy will laugh her head off," he said. He was jubilant now.

"I'm crazy about my family," he said. "My mother and father and my sister and my cousin Kim, they'll laugh their head off."

*"If we just ignore him, maybe he'll go away": bluegills school under a fishing boat, but none of them are falling for that old bait trick.
(Photograph © Doug Stamm/ProPhoto)*

*"Late Night Fishing": an oil painting by Doug Knutson. A native Iowan, Knutson has devoted his painting skills to preserving Midwestern images. (Artwork © Apple Creek Publishing)*

The classic catch of a young angler's first outing: an impressive batch of crappies. *(Photograph © Doug Stamm/ProPhoto)*

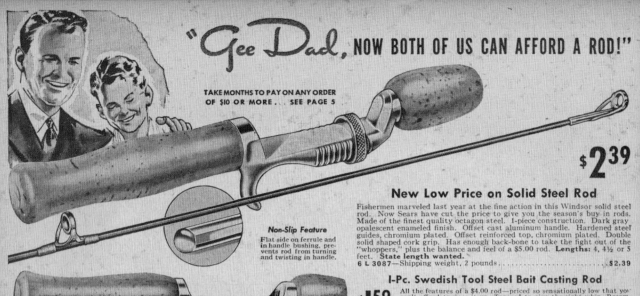

# "Gee Dad, NOW BOTH OF US CAN AFFORD A ROD!"

TAKE MONTHS TO PAY ON ANY ORDER
OF $10 OR MORE . . . SEE PAGE 5

**$2.39**

**Non-Slip Feature**

Flat side on ferrule and
in handle bushing, pre-
vents rod from turning
and twisting in handle.

## New Low Price on Solid Steel Rod

Fishermen marveled last year at the fine action in this Windsor solid steel rod. Now Sears have cut the price to give you the season's buy in rods. Made of the finest quality octagon steel. 1-piece construction. Dark gray opalescent enameled finish. Offset cast aluminum handle. Hardened steel guides, chromium plated. Offset reinforced top, chromium plated. Double solid shaped cork grip. Has enough back-bone to take the fight out of the "whoppers," plus the balance and feel of a $5.00 rod. Lengths: 4, 4½ or 5 feet. State length wanted.
6 L 3087—Shipping weight, 2 pounds.............................$2.39

## 1-Pc. Swedish Tool Steel Bait Casting Rod

**$1.59**

All the features of a $4.00 rod—priced so sensationally low that you can't afford to pass it up. Tapered to give the right whip. Recommended for light casting or trolling. Solid square construction. Cast aluminum offset handle. Brown enameled tip section. Double shaped, solid cork grip. Length: 4 or 4½ ft. State length.
6 L 3088—Shipping weight, 2 pounds............................$1.59

---

## STEEL BAIT CASTING RODS

**(A) GEP'S ACTIONIZED ROD**   **$7.45**
$10.50 Value! Every catch a thrilling experience. 1-piece rod, drawn, seamless tubular steel. Hardened steel guides and top. 4½-ft. has two guides. Gep's B Model offset cast aluminum handle. Vacuum fit, forward grip; shaped cork grip. Medium action. Length: 4½, 5 or 5½ feet. State length.
6 L 3042—Shpg. wt., 2 lbs. 1 oz...$7.45

**(B) TUBULAR CASTING ROD**   **$3.49**
A bait casting rod with the flexibility, feel and look of bamboo, the strength of steel. One-piece—well made from tip to butt, built to last many seasons. Double shaped, solid cork grips as on higher priced rods. Crystal agate guides and top. Length: 4½ or 5 feet. State length wanted.
6 L 3071—Shpg. wt., 1 lb. 6 oz...$3.49

**(C) X-PERT ROD—$10 VALUE**   **$3.89**
Looks like bamboo! Made of fine Swedish tool steel, 1-piece solid construction. Stainless steel guides and reinforced top. Bamboo finish. Offset handle; 1-screw-locking reel seat. Double cork grip. Tip section interlocks so rod cannot turn or twist. Length: 4, 4½ or 5 feet. State length.
6 L 3083—Shpg. wt., 1 lb. 10 oz...$3.89

**(D) NEW HEDDON DE LUXE PAL**   **$12.75**
Hollow cord steel construction. Offset handle. Screw-locking reel seat and top. Light, accurate, powerful and balanced. 'Cork rear grip; walnut forward grip, enameled black. Genuine agate guides. Medium action. Length: 4½ or 5 ft. State length.
6 L 3066—Shpg. wt., 2 lbs. 6 oz.. $12.75

**(E) STREAMLINED—SOLID STEEL**   **$6.49**
Note the beautiful handle . . . new non-fouling guides and tip of stainless steel. Fine Swedish, 1-piece solid steel Octagon shape tip section. Walnut grained finish. Cast aluminum handle highly polished, double solid shaped and tapered cork grips. (Patented.) Length: 4½ or 5 ft. State length.
6 L 3085—Shpg. wt., 1 lb. 14 oz...$6.49

---

### Belmont Split Bamboo Fly Rod   **$4.85**
Here's powerful action plus perfect balance for all-day casting pleasure. Flame finish, 3 pieces with extra tip section. Garnix first guide. Tungsten steel snake guides. Steel tip. Chromium plated mountings. Locking band reel seat. Solid cork grip. Guides and rod wound with silk. Aluminum tip case—guards against breakage. 8½-ft. length, 6-oz. weight or 9-ft. length, 6¼-oz. weight. State length.
6 L 3051—Shipping weight, 1 pound 6 ounces...................$4.85

### Windsor 9-Foot, 3-Piece Split Bamboo   **$3.85**
$5.00 value fly rod! Sturdily constructed, made for either wet or dry fly fishing. Flame finish. Extra tip section. Shaped cork grip. Locking band reel seat. Chrome plated ferrules. Snake guides. Sufficiently powerful to lift a long line out of water with ease. Beautiful appearance, with the stamina and fighting qualities found in higher priced rods.
6 L 3050—Weight of rod, about 5¾ oz. Shpg. wt., 1 lb. 1 oz.....$3.85

### Cane Bamboo Rods at Sears Bargain Prices
Well made and finished. Wire guides, metal top, nickel plated reel seat. Black beaded handle. Ideal rod, used by many fishermen for trolling.
6 L 3034—Mottled Finish.          6 L 3035—Plain Finish.
12-foot, 4 sections.              9½-foot, 3 sections.
Shpg. wt., 1 lb. 11 oz....**$1.59**    Shpg. wt., 1 lb. 8 oz........**98c**

### Sears Low Priced Telescope Bamboo Pole   **39c**
The biggest bargain we could offer in a telescope bamboo pole. Ideal for pan fishing. Light action! 3-piece dark color bamboo; telescopes into two pieces for convenient carrying. Has steel top on tip section. No other mountings. Made in Japan. 3 jointed, telescoped rod.
6 L 3046—12-foot length. Shipping weight, 1 pound.............39c

### STEEL TELESCOPED ROD   **$1.69**
Sears X-Pert! Length extended about 9 ft.; 3 ft. 5 in. telescoped. Solid cork grip. Locking band reel seat. Chrome plated guides, top, mountings. Reversible handle for bait or fly casting.
6 L 3033—Shipping weight, 1 pound............................$1.69

### A BARGAIN "BEAUTY"   **$1.39**
Garnix guides and top. Length, about 9 ft. when extended; telescoped, about 3 ft. Solid ringed cork grip. Nickel plated reel seat and band. Reversible handle for fly or bait angling. Steel telescope, no joints to lose, adjustable for use at any point.
6 L 3004—Shipping weight, 1 pound............................$1.39

---

**22-Pc. $1.50 Value**   **98c**
An ideal set for that boy of yours —take him along on your next fishing trip. This amazing low-price outfit consists of solid steel, 2-joint 43-in. long, bait casting rod; nickel plated bait casting reel; single action; 6 snelled hooks; 12 sinkers; braided cotton line and cork float. Shipping wt., 3 lbs.
6 L 3095.........98c

**$2.50 Value**   **$1.85**
A bargain outfit that has all the equipment needed for trolling, casting or still fishing. 2-piece, 43 inches long solid steel casting rod; 100-yard level-wind quadruple multiplying reel; 25-yard black waterproofed silk line; pocket size tackle box; 6-foot cord stringer; 100 assorted eyed hooks; 6 snelled hooks; 12 sinkers. A big value at this low price.
6 L 3090—Shipping weight, 4 pounds 8 ounces....$1.85

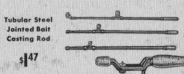

**Tubular Steel Jointed Bait Casting Rod**
**$1.47**
An unusually low price for a rod like this with cast aluminum offset handle! Just the right action for continuous casting. Garnix guides and top. Three-piece rod, independent handle. Has medium light action, is well made and balanced to suit the beginner or experienced bait caster.
6 L 3012—4½-foot length.
Shipping weight, 12 ounces.................................47

47

# MY FIRST FISHING POLE

### By Jimmy Carter

James Earl Carter was the thirty-ninth president of the United States, working in the Oval Office during the years 1976–1980. His service to the country did not end when he lost the presidency to Ronald Reagan in 1980, however. The man from Plains, Georgia, has continued to work for principles in which he believes, including building homes for the less fortunate with Habitat for Humanity International.

Since leaving the White House, Carter has been prolific in writing of his views on everything from politics to aging. Among his varied output are books as diverse as *Keeping Faith: Memoirs of a President* (1982), *The Blood of Abraham: Insights into the Middle East* (1985), *Everything to Gain: Making the Most of the Rest of Your Life* (1987) written with Rosalynn Carter, *Turning Point: A Candidate, a State, and a Nation Come of Age* (1992), and *Always a Reckoning and Other Poems* (1995).

From the days of his youth in Georgia, Carter has always been an avid hunter and fisherman. He reflects on his sporting adventures in his memoir, *An Outdoor Journal* (1988), recounting the day he received his first fishing pole and the world it opened up to him.

*Those were the days. In 1939, the most expensive rod in the Sears Roebuck and Co. catalog was $12.75. As the headline shouted out, "Gee Dad, now both of us can afford a rod!"*

ONE OF THE turning points in my life was when I got my first bait-casting outfit. This purchase, using some of the earnings from my boiled peanut sales, was the culmination of months of desire, conversation, study of outdoor magazines, and comparative analysis of advertisements for rods, reels, and lures. Finally, when I was ready to get serious, I turned to the Sears, Roebuck catalogue and placed my order for a four-foot Shakespeare rod and a Pflueger reel.

When at last the rural mail carrier made the precious delivery, I took a few Heddon and Creek Chub wooden plugs and began to haunt the local millponds in search of largemouth bass. At that time private farm ponds were rare. The millers would permit us to fish in the millponds if our families were among the customers who brought wheat or corn to them to be ground into flour, meal, or grits. Since Daddy spread his business around, there were two or three millponds where my friends and I were welcomed.

We boys would ride our ponies or bicycles the long distances to the mill and, as a necessary courtesy, stop to ask permission to fish in the pond or in the very large pool that almost always formed just below the millrace. The atmosphere inside the mill was fasci-nating, with the great turning pulleys, flat belts driving a multitude of little machines, and the final grain products sifting down at different places from the rotating grinding wheels and oscillating screens. We always stuck our hands into the falling meal, quite hot from the friction of the millstone, and ate with relish. I never ate cold meal in Mama's kitchen or heated any in the stove; it would not have been the same. After a few minutes we were ready to fish, but some of the lonely millers were quite loquacious and had to spend a while talking even with little boys, discussing the weather, giving fishing advice based on recent experience, or idly inquiring about our families.

At the pond we would begin casting, from the shore or from a boat, trying to place the plugs as near as possible to snags, brush, or lily pads where the bass were most likely to be hiding. At first I spent a substantial portion of my time unsnarling backlashes or retrieving my treble-hook bait after an inaccurate cast. My friends and I could not afford to lose a plug. If we hung up too solidly to shake the hooks loose, we would have to ruin a good pool by swimming over to release them.

With practice, while fishing or throwing at a bucket

*Humorous fishing postcard from the 1940s.*

*At home on the bayou: the boat launch at Harmon's Fish Camp on Louisiana's Lake St. John may be a bit weathered, but with these prices, no one can complain. (Photograph © Bill Buckley/The Green Agency)*

in our backyard, I became more and more able to keep the plugs in the water where they belonged. We had good luck fishing this way for bass, because there wasn't much competition. Most fishermen used cane poles and fished deep with worms or minnows, and the per capita use of bait-casting gear was quite low. There was always a great contest between me and my fishing companions over who could catch the most and largest bass. We eagerly tried new plugs whenever they were announced in the fishing and hunting magazines to see if we could improve our catch.

One that proved exceptionally effective was the Hawaiian Wiggler, a metal-headed rubber-skirted plug with a single weedless hook. It seemed to go anywhere

without getting snagged; depending on the model, the arrangement of the skirt, and the speed of retrieval, the lure could be placed at almost any depth we desired. Bass were mesmerized by it. Because the lure rode over the submerged snags, we began to cast increasingly in the creeks, which were filled with logs, limbs, and brush. Although we didn't catch as many fish, the quest was more exciting, as the jack or bass, using submerged hiding places, obstacles, and the current to their advantage, had much more of a fighting chance. Also, there was a greater mystery about what might be found in a deep running stream buried in the shadowy woods than in a man-stocked millpond.

Another lure that added a new dimension to fish-

*The bass is notorious for putting up a tough fight, but he is no match for tough tackle. The reel in this photo is an Eli model made by the William H. Talbot Reel Company of Nevada, Missouri. The split bamboo rod was made by the James Heddon and Sons company of Dowagiac, Michigan. The bass lure on the line is a Baby Seagull made by the Moonlight Bait Company of Michigan. Included here is a mint-condition Bass-Oreno plug and its original box from circa 1920. Made by the renowned South Bend Bait Company of South Bend, Indiana, the Bass-Oreno was "the bait that truly has a wobbling motion," according to the box's advertising line. Memorabilia owners: Pete Press and Guy Chambers. (Photograph © Howard Lambert)*

ing was the Jitterbug, a floating wooden plug with a wide concave tin mouth. When retrieved, it would wobble back and forth and disturb the surface with its antics. We would cast it into a likely place, let it lie still for perhaps half a minute until all the wavelets subsided, and then give it a good twitch or short pull. This would result in the most explosive strikes as the larger bass came up expecting to make a juicy meal of an injured fish, a frog, or some other small animal swimming above its head. The surface wobblers and popping lures were especially effective at night. The powerful thrust of a feeding fish from out of the dark depths, sometimes leaping into the air at my feet or almost under our boat, never failed to startle and thrill me.

About once a year my daddy took me on a fishing trip to a more distant place, usually farther south in Georgia. We made a couple of such visits to the Okefenokee Swamp in the southeastern corner of our state, near the Florida line and not far from the Atlantic Ocean but cut off from the east coast by sand hills. The swamp is a shallow dish of six hundred square miles of water and thousands of islands, mostly of floating peat, on which thick stands of cypress and other trees grow. These peat islands are the "trembling earth" from which the area got its Indian name. Stained with tannin, the water has a reddish-brown color, but was considered by all the fishermen to be pure enough to drink.

We stayed at the only fish camp around the western edge of the swamp, owned by a man named Lem Griffis. His simple pine-board bunkhouses, with screens instead of windowpanes, could accommodate about twenty guests. As we sat around an open fire at night, Lem was always eager to regale us with wild tales about the biggest bear, the prettiest woman, or a catch of so many fish they had to haul in water to fill up the hole left in the lake. His stories were honed by repetition so that the buildup and punch line equaled those of any professional entertainer. We listened and laughed for hours even when we were hearing the same yarn for the second or third time. His regular guests would urge, "Tell us about the city lady who thought her son might drown."

Lem would wait awhile until enough others joined in the request, and then describe in vivid and heart-rending tones the anguish of a mother who was afraid to let her only child near the swamp. "I finally said, 'Ma'am, I can guarantee you the boy won't drown. I've been here all my life and never heerd of anybody drowning in this here swamp.' The lady was quite relieved." There was always a long pause, until Lem finally added, "The 'gators always get them first."

The camp was located near the shore of Billy's Lake, out of which flows the Suwannee River, a beautiful stream that eventually wanders out of Georgia and across the entire Florida peninsula into the Gulf of Mexico. Sometimes we cast or trolled in the lake among the numerous alligators, whose heads would surface quite near us and then submerge quietly as the alligators moved on without a ripple underneath the water. When we inadvertently hooked a small one two or three feet long—we hastily cut our line, trying to save as much of it as possible. We did catch largemouth bass and jack, and quite often had an especially fierce struggle with a mudfish, or bowfin. After such a good fight, we were always disappointed to see what it was, but at Lem's request we would keep some of the largest ones for him to trade off with his neighbors, who liked to eat them.

To me, the most fearsome creature was the alligator gar, a vicious-looking fish with savage teeth. Since we were not fishing with steel leaders, the gar frequently severed our lines. I was almost willing to sacrifice a spoon or other lure in order to avoid having to remove the creatures from my hook and risk losing a finger. They seemed to cruise just under the surface; when one approached the boat we always slapped a paddle in the water to force it to leave. Lem told some frightful stories about the gar fish, and I was inclined to believe him. Later, I checked the fishing encyclopedia and found that the largest alligator gar ever caught was more than ten feet long and weighed 302 pounds. For once, Lem hadn't embellished his descriptions.

We also had good luck still-fishing in Billy's Lake with cane poles for warmouth perch or bream, using pond worms, crawfish tails, or catalpa worms for bait. Most of the time, however, we preferred to go into the more remote wilderness areas of the Okefenokee. Lem's sons were our guides as we moved deep into the swamp each day. Our boats were long and narrow, specially built to squeeze between the snags and cypress roots along the water trails that had been chopped out to connect the numerous small open places among the

*Many fish species dwell among the reeds; therefore, many anglers dwell there, too. (Photograph © Richard Hamilton Smith)*

*Anglers fish for largemouth bass amidst a swamp of cypress trees. (Photograph © Bill Buckley/The Green Agency)*

trees. Because a very slow but steady current moved throughout the swamp toward Billy's Lake, there was no stagnant water there. Fish were plentiful and we caught a lot of them, but one of the attractions of the trip was to see Lem's sons use a casting rod. Whenever we stopped on one of the floating islands for lunch, they would take the boat a short distance from shore and, on each cast, place the lures within an inch or two of their chosen target point, underneath an overhanging bush, between the roots, or among the lily pads. They knew just what hat kind of lure action would appeal to a fish, and it was amazing to see how quickly they caught enough bass for all of us to eat.

As we moved along these waterways we saw many kinds of birds, including ducks, terns, herons, egrets, ibises, kingfishers, hawks, pileated woodpeckers, and on rare occasions, a bald eagle. The reflection on the surface of the still, dark water was practically perfect, and in some of our photographs it was later impossible to tell which side was up or down. When we were still, the silence would at first seem absolute, but then we would begin to hear a myriad of sounds coming from the surrounding swamp. The Griffis boys could identify the cry of each bird and animal. I remember particularly the bellow of the bull alligators and the deathly silence that for a few moments always followed.

Late one afternoon, one of the other guest fishermen shot an enormous snapping turtle and brought it back to camp. Lem and his boys hung it up on a tree limb and dressed it, easily removing the edible portions by running a sharp knife around the inside edge of the ridged shell. After cutting up the choice-looking meat into small pieces, we set a large washpot half-filled with water on the campfire and added the turtle, two or three chickens, some onions, and later a few vegetables and seasoning. In a couple of hours we all ate several bowlfuls of the turtle soup, a supper few of us would ever forget.

We returned home from the Okefenokee with enough cleaned and iced fish to supply all our kinfolks and neighbors. Sometimes Daddy would take a portion of our catch to the freezer locker in Plains to be kept for a future party and fish fry for his friends. One of my favorite aspects of each trip was telling Mama and my sisters about my part for a few days in a man's world. I proudly described our experiences, most of

them not needing much enhancing to make them interesting.

A few miles north of the Okefenokee was the small village of Hortense, not far from where the Little Satilla River joins the Big Satilla. This was one of my father's favorite fishing spots; he tried to go there every year with some of his associates in the farming, peanut, and fertilizer business. On two occasions he took me with him, when I was about ten or twelve years old. We stayed in a big and somewhat dilapidated wood-frame house on a small farm near the banks of the Little Satilla. The house had been built to accommodate at least three generations of a family, but now there were just a man named Joe Strickland, his wife, Shug, and two daughters, one a pretty girl in her teens named Jessie. Joe was the guide for our group of about six people. The women cooked our meals and plowed mules in the small fields during the day while we were fishing. It was the first time I had seen women plowing, which I found quite surprising, but they all seemed to take it as a matter of course.

The Little Satilla is a serpentine stream in the flattest part of Georgia's coastal plain, weaving back and forth from one bend to another. A number of oxbow lakes had been left behind when the river changed its course. We fished in the area of what was called Ludie's Lake. On the outside of almost every bend of the stream there was a deep hole, often cut into a steep bank, and on the opposite side of the river was usually a sand bar. There were not as many bushes and snags in the water as we had around Plains, and the bottom was sandy and firm.

I had never done this kind of fishing before. We spent our time in the stream, wading halfway across it to fish in the deep water under the overhanging banks, using the longest cane poles we could handle. I wore cutoff overall pants with no shirt, and tied my fish stringer to one of the belt loops. Joe and I were the only ones barefoot; all the other men had on old tennis shoes or brogans to protect their tender feet. We fished with large pond worms and caught mostly "copperheads," which were very large bluegill bream whose heads, when mature, assumed a bronze color, perhaps from the tannin stain in the water.

The group of us would string out along the river,

my daddy and I usually fishing within sight of each other. We always had a fairly good idea of what luck each fisherman was having. For some reason I have never understood, the men would shout "Billy McKay!" when they had on a nice fish. The words would roll through the woods as all of us smiled; the enthusiasm of the voices was contagious. Each night after supper I went to bed early, but the men stayed up to play poker and to have a few drinks. Sometimes they made enough noise to wake me up, but I didn't mind. It seemed to make me more a member of the party if they weren't trying to stay quiet just for me. Most often I was tired enough to go right back to sleep.

While we were in the river Joe moved quietly from one of us to another, just to make sure we were properly spaced and to give advice about the water and some of the bypasses we had to take around obstacles. He tried—successfully—to build up a reputation as something of a character and always gave the group something to talk about during the months between our visits to Hortense.

Once we were walking single file along a path toward the river and Joe called, "Watch out for the barbed wire!"

One of the men said, "Joe, you didn't look down. How do you know wire's there?"

Joe said, "My feet will flatten briers or thorns, but I can feel barbed wire when I step on it."

Another time, when we had to cross the river, Joe walked down the bank, entered the water with his pole and lunch over his head, and moved smoothly across toward the other side with the water never higher than his armpits. The next man, whom I called Mr. Charlie, was the oldest in the group, and he stepped off in the water and immediately went down out of sight. He came up sputtering, and shouted, "Joe, how deep is it here?"

Joe replied, "Oh, I reckon it's about fifteen foot." Joe could tread water like a duck, and just wanted to demonstrate his prowess so that none of us would forget.

Then came my most memorable day. Late one afternoon, after a good day of fishing, Daddy called me over and asked me to keep his string of fish while he went up the river to talk to one of his friends. I tied it

on with mine on the downstream side of me while I kept fishing, enjoying the steady pull of the current on our day's catch. It wasn't long before I watched my cork begin to move slowly and steadily up under a snag and knew I had hooked a big one. After a few minutes I had a large copperhead bream in my hands, but as I struggled with it and wondered how I was going to hold the fish while untying the stringer, a cold chill went down my spine. I realized that the tugging of the current on the stringers was gone, as were all our fish! My belt loop had broken.

I threw my pole up on the nearest sand bar and began to dive madly into the river below where I had been standing.

Then I heard Daddy's voice calling my nickname, "Hot," he said, "what's wrong?"

"I've lost the fish, Daddy."

"All of them? Mine too?"

"Yes, sir." I began to cry, and the tears and water ran down my face together each time I came up for breath.

Daddy was rarely patient with foolishness or mistakes. But after a long silence, he said, "Let them go." I stumbled out on the bank, and he put his arms around me.

It seems foolish now, but at that time it was a great tragedy for me. We stood there for a while, and he said, "There are a lot more fish in the river. We'll get them tomorrow." He knew how I felt and was especially nice to me for the next couple of days. I worshipped him.

At Joe's home we ate fish and whatever was in season. Both times I went, our breakfasts consisted of biscuits, grits, green beans, and fried fish. It was the first time I had eaten green beans early in the morning, but soon it seemed like a normal thing to do. With plenty of butter and sugar-cane syrup to go with the piles of hot biscuits, we never got up from the table hungry.

When I left Joe's place to come home, his daughter Jessie told me that she had brought me a going-away present. She then handed me a baby alligator about a foot long, whom I immediately named Mickey Mouse. When I returned to our house I installed him inside a large truck tire, partially buried in the ground and covered with boards. For a number of weeks I fed him earthworms, crickets, wasp larvae, and anything else he

*1940s postcard: "Here You Learn How To Fish!"*

would eat. My friends were quite envious of my new pet. Unfortunately, the cats and dogs around the farm were also interested. One morning I went out to feed Mickey and found the boards pushed aside and the little alligator missing. Daddy was very considerate and said he was sure the 'gator had escaped into the nearest swamp. I was not quite naive enough to believe him, but from then on I stayed on the lookout for my 'gator whenever I was fishing or exploring along the neighborhood creeks.

Almost fifty years later, after I left the White House, I stopped by Hortense, Georgia, to try to find the place we used to visit. I couldn't remember the roads or even Joe's last name when I inquired of some folks in the service station. I did recall the pretty daughter, but one of the men told me: "We had a lot of pretty daughters around here." At least I remembered the bare feet, barbed wire, good catches, lost fish, Mickey Mouse, and green beans for breakfast. When I described some of these

things to the postmistress, she said, "You must mean Joe Strickland. Miss Jessie still lives at the same place, but in a new house." I followed her directions and found the cottage in what had been the large yard of the old house, just a few steps from the Little Satilla River.

Miss Jessie responded to our knock on her door, saying, "Won't y'all come in!" even before she knew who we were. We had a good time reminiscing about old times. Both her parents had died long ago, and she was intrigued that I remembered so much about them. She said she remembered my visits: "I told a lot of people while you were in the White House that the President had fished with my daddy."

To which I replied, "When I was in the White House, I told several people the same thing about yours. Many of the most highly publicized events of my presidency are not nearly as memorable or significant in my life as fishing with my daddy and yours when I was a boy. Certainly, almost none of them was as enjoyable!"

*Working in his shop, rodmaker Glenn Brackett fashions a bamboo flyrod for the prestigious firm of R. L. Winton Rod Company.*

## The Fine Art of Handcrafting a Fly Rod

"It took me fifteen minutes the other day to memorize the name of my new casting rod, and I've already forgotten it. When I was younger, we didn't have to memorize the names of our rods because we didn't have any. We had what were called "fish poles." Even now, after nearly forty years, I will still occasionally refer to a three-hundred-dollar custom-built fly rod as a "fish pole."

—Patrick F. McManus,
"*Fish Poles*, and Other Useful Terminology"

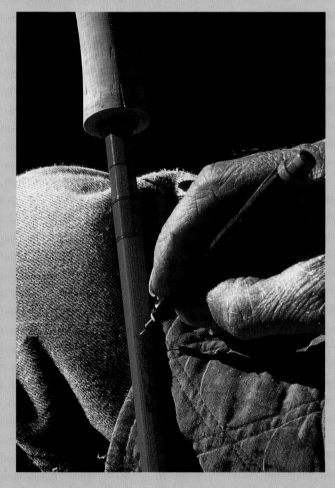

*To hold the six sections of bamboo together during the gluing process, Bracket winds the rod with cotton line. When the glue is dry, the line will be unwound before the rod is fine sanded.*

*The rodmaker signs his work. (Photographs © Dale C. Spartas / The Green Agency)*

# CLYDE:
# THE METAMORPHOSIS

By Nick Lyons

Few people know fishing literature like Nick Lyons. A former professor of English at Hunter College in New York City, Lyons blended his love of angling with his knowledge of literature to create the publishing house Lyons & Burford, later known simply as the Lyons Press. His company has published books and anthologies collecting together the stories of many of the greatest writers who have ever been handy with a pen as well as a rod and reel.

Lyons himself is also a prolific writer on the subject of angling. He has authored numerous articles and books on the subject, including *Bright Rivers* (1977), *Confessions of a Fly Fishing Addict* (1989), *Spring Creek* (1992), and *In Praise of Wild Trout* (1998), among many others.

In this grand jest in the style of Franz Kafka, Lyons writes with a unique sense of humor about a subject near and dear to his heart.

*A fly fisher's dream: a brook trout making a dramatic leap from the water as it struggles with the end of the line. (Photograph © Doug Stamm/ProPhoto)*

MY FRIEND CLYDE awoke one morning from uneasy dreams to find himself transformed in the night into a gigantic brown trout. It was no joke. He looked around him, hoping to see his pleasant little one-room apartment where he had lived a hermetic life since his wife cashiered him. Its walls were papered with color photographs of rising trout and natural flies the size of grouse; each corner held three or four bamboo rods in aluminum tubes; the chests of drawers were crammed with blue-dun necks and flies and fly boxes and his thirteen Princess reels; the windowsills and bookcases were packed solid with hundreds of books and catalogs and magazines devoted to the sport to which he had devoted his life. They were not there. Neither were his hands, which were fins.

Instead, he was suspended in cold moving water under an old upturned maple stump. From the clarity and size of the water, he deduced he was in Montana, or perhaps Idaho. That was fine with Clyde. If he was going to be a trout, and he had often meditated on what it would be like to be a trout (so he could tell how they thought), he'd just as well be one in Montana and Idaho.

"Well, this love of fly fishing sure takes me places I otherwise wouldn't go," he thought.

And as soon as he thought this, he realized, since he was thinking, that he had resolved an age-old problem. If he, existing under that old tree stump, could think, he could analyze his own thoughts; and since what was true for him would have to be true for all trout, he could learn what any trout thought. He was glad he had read Descartes and Kant before he went on the Halford binge.

Curiously, his esoteric studies had led him closer and closer to this point. Only the night before he had been sitting in the dimly lit room, sunk deep into his armchair in front of the lit fish-tank in which swam Oscar, his pet brown. He had been staring intently, reciting a mantra, meditating, as he did every night for four hours, when, for a moment—no, it could not be true—Oscar had (at least he thought so) told him that Foolex dubbing was the ultimate solution to the body problem. "Not quill ribbing?" he had asked audibly. "Definitely not," said Oscar. "I like you so I'll give you the straight poop: Foolex is where it's at. Anyway, tomorrow it . . . oh, you'll find out."

And so he had.

He had a thousand questions and worked his way a bit upstream, where he saw a pretty spotted tail waving gently back and forth. The trout, a hen, about three pounds, shifted slightly as Clyde nudged her and eyed him suspiciously: it was still three weeks before spawning season and she was feeling none too frisky. He opened his mouth to ask her about Foolex bodies and careened back in the current. The henfish, named Trudy, thought he was a dumb cluck and that she ought to work her way quickly past the riffle into the upper pool. Maybe this bird's clock was wrong; though she had a rotten headache, he might even attack her.

Clyde, ever watchful, immediately deduced from her defensiveness that communication among trout, like communication between fly fishermen and bocce players, was impossible. He'd have to answer his questions by himself. This is never easy, particularly not on an empty stomach. He had not eaten anything since the pepperoni sandwich fifteen hours earlier; and he was not dumb enough to think he could soon get another, since the Belle Deli was two thousand miles away.

There was a silver flash and Clyde turned and shot up after it, turning on it as it slowed and turned and lifted up in the current. But he was too late. A little twelve-inch rainbow had sped from behind a large rock and grasped the thing, and it was now struggling with ludicrous futility across stream, the silver object stuck in its lower jaw.

"Incredible!" Clyde thought. "How could I have been so dumb?" He had not seen the hooks; he had not distinguished between metal and true scales. If he who had studied Halford, Skues, Marinaro, and Schwiebert could not distinguish a C. P. Swing from a dace tartare, what hope had any of his speckled kin? He shivered with fear as he asked himself: "Are *all* trout this dumb?"

He worked his way back under the upturned stump, into the eddy, and sulked. This was a grim business. He noticed he was trembling with acute anxiety neurosis but could not yet accept that *all* trout were neurotic. He was positively starved now and would have risen to spinach, which he hated.

Bits and pieces of debris, empty nymph shucks, a couple of grubs swept into the eddy. He nosed them, bumped them, took them into his mouth, spit some of them out. By noon he had managed to nudge loose one half-dead stone-fly nymph, *Pteronarcys californica;*

*Despite a coating of snow and the advent of winter, a diehard fly fisherman wades into Oregon's Crooked River for one last chance at an elusive trout. (Photograph © Dennis Frates)*

he had nabbed one measly earthworm; and he had found a few cased caddises. Most food, he noted, came off the bottom; that's where it was at. The lure had come down from the surface; he should have known. He was learning something new every minute.

By now he had recognized that he was in the Big Hole River, below Divide; he was sure he had once fished the pool. Settled into that eddy under the stump, he now knew why he had not raised a fish here: the current swung the food down below the undercut bank, but his flies had been too high up in the water. The way to fish this run was almost directly downstream from his present position, casting parallel to the bank so the nymph would have a chance to ride low and slip down into the eddy.

He was trying to plot the physics of the thing, from below, and was getting dizzy, when he realized he could starve flat down to death if he didn't stop trying to be

a trout fisherman and settle for being a trout. His stomach felt pinched and dry; his jaws ached to clamp down on a fresh stone-fly nymph or, yes, a grasshopper. That's what he wanted. He suddenly had a mad letch for grasshoppers—and there was absolutely nothing he could do to get one. He was totally dependent on chance. "A trout's lot," he thought, "is not a happy one."

Just then the surface rippled a bit, perhaps from a breeze, and a couple of yards upstream, he saw the tell-tale yellow body, kicking legs, and molded head of a grasshopper. It was August, and he knew the grasshoppers grew large around the Big Hole at that time of the year. It came at him quickly, he rose sharply to it, then stopped and turned away with a smirk. "Not me. Uh–uh. A Dave's Hopper if I ever saw one. Not for this guy." And as he thought this, Trudy swept downstream past him, too quick for him to warn, and nabbed the thing in an abrupt little splash. Then she turned, swam up by

ABOVE: *Dwarfed by the Colorado mountains, an angler plies a pool in a glistening stream. (Photograph © Gary A. McVicker)*

LEFT: *A fuzzy-tailed fly catches the eye of a steelhead, causing it to veer sharply from its path. (Photograph © Doug Stamm/ProPhoto)*

*"A trout is a gentleman, and should be treated as such. . . ." —Charles Bradford, "Trout Truths" (Photograph © Alan and Sandy Carey)*

him, seemed to shake her head and say, "How dumb a cluck can you be?"

So it *had* been the real thing. Nature was imitating art now. Oh, he could taste the succulent hopper.

Another splatted down, juicy and alive, and he rose again, paused, and it shot downstream in a rush. He'd never know about that one.

Oh, the existential torment of it! "And I thought deciding which artificial fly to use was hard!"

Two more hoppers, then a third splatted down. He passed up one, lost a fin-race with Trudy for the third. She was becoming a pill.

He could bear it no longer. He'd even eat a Nick's Crazylegs if it came down. Anything. Anything to be done with the torment, the veil of unknowing, the inscrutability, which was worse than the pain in his gut, as it always is.

And then he saw it.

It was a huge, preposterous, feathered thing with a big black hook curled up under it. Some joker with three thumbs had thought it looked like a grasshopper. The body was made of Foolex. How could Oscar possibly have thought that body anything other than insulting? Clyde's hook jaw turned up in a wry smile; he wiggled his adipose fin. The fly came down over him and he watched it safely from his eddy. And it came down again. Then again. Twelve. Thirteen times. Trudy had moved twice in its direction. He could tell she was getting fairly neurotic about it.

Foolex? That body could not fool an imbecile. It *was* an insult!

Eighteen. Twenty times the monstrosity came over him. He was fuming now. How *dare* someone throw something like that at him! Had they no respect whatsoever? If that's all fishermen thought of him, what did it matter. He was bored and hungry and suffering from a severe case of *angst* and humiliation. Nothing mattered. It was a trout's life.

He rose quickly and surely now, turning as the thing swept past him on the thirty-third cast. He saw it hang in the surface eddy for a moment. He opened his mouth. Foolex? It infuriated him! It was the ultimate insult.

He lunged forward. And at the precise moment he knew exactly what trout see and why they strike, he stopped being a trout.

# AS THE WORM SQUIRMS

## By Patrick F. McManus

As America's favorite outdoors humorist, Patrick F. McManus has few peers. He writes in a jocular, over-the-top style that blends the irony of Mark Twain with the bravado of Ernest Hemingway to create tall tales that are pure McManus.

McManus's stories appear regularly in sports magazines, including *Field & Stream*, and detail his misadventures with every type of outdoors sport imaginable. He has more than ten books in print, including *A Fine and Pleasant Misery* (1981), *They Shoot Canoes, Don't They?* (1982), *Real Ponies Don't Go Oink!* (1991), *The Good Samaritan Strikes Again* (1992), *How I Got This Way* (1994), and *Into The Twilight, Endlessly Grousing* (1997). He also published a collection of recipes and reminiscences entitled *Whatchagot Stew: A Memoir of an Idaho Childhood, with Recipes and Commentaries* (1991) written with his sister, Patricia "The Troll" McManus Gass.

This story from *The Night The Bear Ate Goombaw* (1989) is prime McManus, a fishing soap opera that all anglers can appreciate.

*Indeed there is money in worms, as these advertisements from the first half of the twentieth century prove.*

I WAS UP AT my cabin the other day, when young Lonnie Bird stopped by to show me a seven-pound bass he had just caught in the river. A s-e-v-e-n-p-o-u-n-d bass! Never had I seen such a bass taken out of the river, the very same river that for twenty years I had beaten to a froth from mouth to source with every lure known to man and never landed a bass over two pounds. My head reeled at the sight of the thing. From *my* river! A *SEVEN-POUND* BASS! I had to force myself to breathe. My whole life as an angler flashed before my eyes, and I thought I must surely be dying from the mere sight of this finny miracle.

"Not a bad fish, Lonnie," I said. "Where'd you catch him?"

"Up in Crawford Slough. You know where those submerged stumps are at the head of the slough?"

*Crawford Slough! Cripes! The submerged stumps! Oh, the pain! I can't stand the pain of it!* "Uh-hunh. Crawford Slough. Well, you got yourself a pretty nice fish there, Lonnie. Probably caught it on a crank bait, right?"

"Nope, a worm."

*A worm! Of course! Why didn't I think of that? Aaaaiiii!* "Yes, I've found that some of the larger bass will go for a worm this time of year. I bet it was a purple silver-flaked worm with a gray tail. Right?"

"Nope. A real worm."

"What do you mean, a real worm?"

"I mean a real worm, one that ain't plastic."

"Aha! The kind of worm that you dig . . ."

"Yeah, the kind that you buy in the little round paper cartons out of the dairy food section at the Super Mart."

"Oh, that kind of real worm. Well, to tell you the truth, Lonnie, I feel it's much more sporting to use artificial worms. I would have to be pretty hard up for bass before I would resort to fishing with live worms I bought out of the dairy section at the Super Mart."

"Won't do you no good to rush in there after a carton of them, because I bought the last of the Super Mart's worms this morning. The early bird gets the worms! Ha! Get it?"

"Yeah, I get it, you glutton, you hoarder of worms! Listen, I'll give you a buck for a dozen worms right now, no questions asked."

"Nope. By the time the worm man comes around to the Super Mart again, I'll have caught all the seven-pound bass out of Crawford Slough!"

"Okay, Lonnie, I'll show you. I'll just go dig my own worms."

"Dig your own? What do you mean, dig your own? You think worms just grow in the ground? Worms come in round paper cartons from big worm ranches. Everybody knows that. Shoot, if you could just dig 'em out of the ground, the worm man would go bust."

As soon as Lonnie had departed with his monstrous bass, I grabbed a shovel and spaded up an acre of ground. Not a single worm put in an appearance.

The following week I was waiting at the Super Mart for the worm man to bring in a fresh shipment. A late-model pickup truck drove up and a tall, lanky gentleman got out. He was wearing cowboy boots, a ten-gallon hat, and a nice leather vest. He lifted a crate of little round paper cartons from the back of the pickup.

"You must be the worm man," I said.

"Actually, I prefer to be known as a worm rancher," he said frostily.

"I'm sorry," I said. "I should have known—the boots, the hat. How big's your ranch?"

"Almost half an acre."

"Half an acre," I said. "Well, I suppose you can raise quite a few worms on half an acre."

"Yep. Right now I'm runnin' three hundred thousand head on the north pasture alone."

"Wow! How big's the north pasture?"

"About this big, give or take a couple of inches. Most of the stock's out on the open range, though. You might like to come out and watch the roundup."

"A roundup! How many hands does it take for a roundup?"

"Six usually. Mine, my wife's, and my son Grover's."

"Sounds exciting," I said. "It would be worth the trip just to see the itty-bitty branding iron. For right now, though, I'd just like to buy some worms off you."

"Shore thing, podner. How many you want?"

"Oh, about fifty head."

While the worm rancher was counting out my purchase, I started wondering whatever happened to regular old worms, the kind you dig out of the ground rather than out of the dairy case at a grocery store—ranch-raised worms. I'll admit that I'm glad to see the resurgence of worms, whatever their source. For a while, I thought they might have disappeared forever. I re-

*An angler fishes a favorite hole as the first rays of the morning sun filter through the trees lining Minnesota's Pickerel Lake. (Photograph © Richard Hamilton Smith)*

member going through the miniature-marshmallow phase of fish bait. It was disgusting. Pastel marshmallows! Remember? Arguments would break out over what was the best marshmallow bait, the pinks or the greenies. True anglers were ashamed to walk into a store and buy a package of pastel miniature marshmallows. "My little boy likes to eat them," you'd say to the clerk. "Yeah, sure," she'd say. "And my dog, Rex, plays the violin." Or maybe some other anglers would ask you what you caught your fish on, and you'd say a No. 16 Royal Coachman on a one-ounce tippet, and about then a miniature pink marshmallow would fall out of your fishing vest and bounce up and down on the dock like a Super Ball. And you would squish it with your foot, but it would be too late. What I hated most about bait marshmallows was that they wouldn't sink when they came off the hook. Soon there would be these rainbow waves of miniature marshmallow slopping around the lake. They were pretty, yes, but they lacked that gritty, smelly, slimy essence that true fishermen love about real fish bait.

Next came the canned-corn phase. Not just any canned corn would do either. It had to be white niblet corn. On opening day of fishing season, five thousand fishermen would descend on a little lake near my home, and every one of them would have his little can of white niblet corn. Some of the anglers would actually open the cans of corn at home on electric can openers! They were despised by the corn purists, who insisted on hacking open the can with a dull jackknife. Unlike marshmallows, the niblets of corn sank when they came off the hook. After the first couple weeks of fishing season, the bottom of the lake would be covered with fermenting corn. Toward the end of summer, the lake approached 85 proof. The perch were already pickled when you caught them. They would lie on their backs in the live well, hiccuping.

White niblet corn and miniature pastel marshmallows were enough to give an old-time wormer like myself the galloping shudders. Kids would go into a store and buy marshmallows and corn and think that was all there ever was to getting bait. When I was a boy, catching worms was more of a challenge than catching fish. Some of our worms were bigger than most of our fish. We bragged about big worms we had dug. We lied about bigger worms we hadn't dug. We were worm snobs. Artificial flies were for sissies. We'd ridicule a kid right off the creek for fishing a dry fly. "Whatsa matter," we'd say, "scared of worms?"

I was a good wormer, but not a great one. Dum-dum Harris was a great wormer—the best! If there had been an Olympic event for worming, Dum-dum would have taken the gold. He wasn't all that bright about most things. He'd been in fourth grade longer than most of us had been in school. The teacher thought of him almost as part of the woodwork. Once she tried to screw a pencil sharpener onto his chest. Dum-dum helped her! But he was a genius when it came to finding worms.

Toward the end of July, the clay soil in our part of the country would bake into one great ceramic tile. Once you had chipped through the tile, you would start shoveling your way toward China. It took you so long to dig down to moist earth, where a worm might

possibly be, that by the time you discovered you'd dug a dry hole, it was too late to dig another. If you managed to find one worm, you could go fishing for a couple of hours, pinching little sections off him to rebait the hook. Finally, you would be down to one little half-inch section of worm, and you and your buddy would be fighting to see who got it. Then Dum-dum would show up. He would actually fish whole worms. If a worm got even a little soggy, he would toss it into the creek and bait up another one. Dum-dum was the first person I ever saw practice conspicuous consumption.

Finally, by August, the rest of the boys would be down to fishing with manure-pile worms, tiny, pale, squiggly things. Dum-dum would come along with a can overflowing with big fat night crawlers.

"Mighty sick-looking worms you got there," he'd say, flipping out a half-pound night crawler.

"Yeah," one of us would reply. "Well, you'd be sick-looking too, if you were raised in a manure pile."

Sometimes Dum-dum would take mercy on us. "C'mon, Dum-dum, give us some worms," we'd beg.

*The morning sun rises over the old fishing hole. (Photograph © Jack Bissell)*

*Working by the light of a camp lantern, fly fishermen tie flies for the next day's outing. (Photograph © Bill Buckley/The Green Agency)*

*A fly fisherman's patient efforts in a Rocky Mountain stream are rewarded with a healthy rainbow trout. (Photograph © Alan and Sandy Carey)*

"We dug up half the county and didn't find a single worm."

"Got just enough for myself," he'd say. "But I'll help you find some."

Then he'd turn around and look this way and that, studying various clods of dirt. After a bit, he would walk over to a clod and pull it up, revealing a whole convention of worms. Dum-dum, however, didn't perform this service free of charge. Usually it would cost us our school hot-lunch desserts until about next Easter. We could scarcely believe we had frittered away the easy worms of May and June and were now forced to pay loan-shark prices to Dum-dum.

One of the advantages of worming, we discovered early on, was that it discouraged little girls from wanting to go fishing with us. When we got to be sixteen, however, we learned that it also discouraged big girls from wanting to go fishing with us. Most of us switched to flies then, claiming that worms really weren't a sporting bait. After thirty years and more of fishing with flies and other artificial lures, few things would make me return to worms. One of them is a seven-pound bass that may have escaped Lonnie Bird up at Crawford Slough.

After the worm rancher had stacked up my little round paper cartons of fifty worms, I pulled out a couple dollar bills and asked him how much I owed him.

"Let's see," he said, scratching his head. "This is always the hard part. What's fifty cents times fifty? Shoot, I'll go get my calculator."

"Hey, don't bother," I said. "That works out to twenty-five dollars."

"It does? Okay, I'll take your word for it. That'll be twenty-five dollars."

"Twenty-five dollars!" I screamed. "That's fifty cents a worm!"

"Yep," he said, grinning. "Or you could pay me all your hot-lunch desserts up until next Easter."

"What?" I said. "Dum-dum? My gosh, it is you—Dum-dum Harris!"

I don't know why I hadn't recognized him right off. Not that many people go around with a pencil sharpener screwed to their chest.

# A FLY FISHING LIFE

### By Joan Salvato Wulff

Joan Salvato Wulff is a magician with a fly rod. She began fly fishing when she was a mere ten years old under the sage tutelage of her father. Since then, she has won seventeen national casting titles, and holds the International Women's Fishing Association records for brook trout and Atlantic salmon.

Long regarded as one of the best fly-fishing instructors anywhere, Wulf's expertise has brought renown to her internationally known fly-fishing school in Lew Beach, New York. Along with her regular fly-casting column for *Fly Rod & Reel* magazine, she has authored three books that delve into the finer points of fly fishing, *Joan Wulff's Fly Casting Techniques* (1987), *Joan Wulff's Fly-Casting Accuracy* (1997), and *Joan Wulff's Fly Fishing: Expert Advice from a Woman's Perspective* (1991).

This excerpt from *Joan Wulff's Fly Fishing* tells of the influences in her life that have inspired her deep-rooted fascination with the craft.

*Minnesota artist Bob White captures the peace of a fall fly fishing outing in his watercolor painting "Autumn Afternoon."*

As is true of many of the women of my generation who fly fish, my father was a fly fisherman. Mother was not. It became apparent the first time I accompanied them for an evening of fly fishing for bass that Dad had all the fun while Mom got yelled at for not keeping the rowboat at the right distance from bass cover. Unencumbered by the knowledge that women didn't fish, it was obvious to me then, at age five or six, that it was better to be the fisherman than the rower.

My dad, Jimmy Salvato, gave up an accounting job in his mid-twenties to become the proprietor of the Paterson Rod and Gun Store. Despite a seventy-hour work week, he wrote an outdoor column for the *Paterson Morning Call,* helped to start most of the conservation clubs in northern New Jersey, hunted moose and woodcock, raised hunting dogs, and managed to fit in some tournament casting on summer Sundays.

The Paterson Casting Club met at the Oldham Pond near our home in North Haledon, and when the older of my two brothers, Jimmy, reached the age of eight, he went along with Dad to the club's practice sessions. Joan, who was ten, was bypassed.

I *wanted* to fly cast. Gaining Mom's permission to try it with Dad's fly rod one afternoon, I went to the casting club dock, put the rod together and flailed away. *Oops!* The tip and butt sections separated and, with no fly on the leader to stop it, the tip went into the six-foot-deep pond water. Home I went, crying and afraid of my father's anger. Mom may have been, too, because when our next-door neighbor came home from work, an hour before Dad would come in for dinner, she asked for his help. We went back to the dock with a garden rake and, bless Mr. Kuehn, he snagged it in a few minutes.

The Dad I didn't know very well, the authoritarian figure in my life, the man of whom I was a little bit afraid, asked me to join him and Jimmy the next Sunday at the casting club.

I can look back now and say I was born to fly cast. While it wasn't easy, I was drawn to it. That same year (1937) a friend, Eleanor Egg, had talked my parents into letting me take tap, ballet, and acrobatic lessons from her. I am convinced that the dancing lessons improved my casting because they taught me to use my whole body to back up my limited ten-year-old strength.

Casting and dancing became my favorite pastimes. I won my first casting title in 1938, the New Jersey Sub-Junior All Around Championship, and with it gained the motivation to practice. Although I took college preparatory courses in high school, when my guidance counsellor asked what my plans were ("I don't know") and what I liked to do ("fly cast and dance"), she suggested secretarial school.

I had started to teach tap dancing when I was thirteen and by the time I took my first job as a junior secretary with N.W. Ayer & Sons, an advertising agency in New York City, for $25 per week, I was earning $20 for teaching dancing on Saturdays. Just before I turned eighteen I gave up secretarial work for dancing and opened a school with Eleanor. How lucky I was! She instilled in me the joy of living, and of teaching, and we had a perfect partnership for eight years. I taught dancing for ten months of the year and competed as an amateur in five or six casting tournaments during the two summer months.

Between 1943 and 1951 I won one or more national women's titles every year and, in 1951, garnered four plus a fisherman's distance fly event against all-male competition. I beat the second-place winner—my boyfriend, Johnny Dieckman—by an average of one-third of a foot! This was an event in which I could master the tackle as well as the men because it was limited to what we now call a 9-weight line.

Distance fly casting had become my real love in tournaments. There were two distance fly events, the one mentioned above, with tackle suitable for actual fishing, and a second, the "unrestricted" trout fly event, with specialty tackle capable of making casts so long as to be impractical for a fisherman. The event, which is still included in casting competitions, challenges casters to design tackle and develop techniques to cast a fly as far as is humanly possible with a one-handed rod. Interestingly, the average fly angler does benefit. The shooting-head line and the double-haul casting technique were either developed or refined through tournaments.

I had begun by "ghillying" for my casting mentor,

*With Dad's rod and reel in hand, this little girl is ready to tackle the big fish. (Photograph © Bill Buckley/The Green Agency)*

*A solitary angler fishes Idaho's Silver
Creek on a glorious late autumn day.
(Photograph © William H. Mullins)*

ABOVE: *The sign of a veteran angler: a well-worn cowboy hat pierced by the owner's favorite flies. (Photograph © Mark Kayser)*

FACING PAGE: *As if it could defy gravity, a salmon jumps up a waterfall. (Photograph © Len Rue Jr.)*

William Taylor. After each cast I pulled the dozens of yards of shooting line back in from the water and spread them out on the dock beside him. I came to appreciate that distance fly casting was a sport of beautiful form and motion, requiring the use of the whole body. In 1947 I could no longer resist trying it, but I found Bill's tackle too heavy and so he made a lighter rod for me. Lighter? It weighed 6¾ ounces! (We had only bamboo to use then.)

For this event the silk line was specially constructed, by hand, of spliced sections of line of different diameters to form a taper. This tapered "head" was approximately fifty-two feet long and had a weight limitation of 1½ ounces. It was backed by monofilament shooting line and the record casts were 150 feet and up. I could not cast a line that heavy, so, once again, Bill Taylor made me a "lighter" one. It weighed 1⅜ ounces.

Even at those weights I could not false cast the

outfit. I didn't have the strength to maintain line speed on a false cast, so all of my distance casting was done by taking the line off the water (with the head out of the rod tip), shooting on the backcast, and shooting the rest on the forward cast. In spite of my lack of strength, my coordination and timing allowed me to place about halfway down the line among the male competitors in most tournaments.

The longest cast I ever made in a national tournament was 144 feet, but in a registered New Jersey state tournament in 1960 I cast my fly 161 feet for an unofficial women's record. Unofficial because there weren't any, or enough, other women distance casters to have an event of our own. The men's record was less than 190 feet. Oh, that I could do it all again with graphite!

In 1948 fly casting brought me to the attention of angler, author, and famous hotelier Charles Ritz at a sportsmen's show in New York. Charles invited me to

compete in the French National Tournament in Paris and in the International Casting Tournament in London, the first events of their kind to be held after the war. I won the International ⅝-ounce plug-casting championship, competing against men and women, professionals and amateurs.

Our dancing school, meanwhile, had become very successful. In 1952 I decided to leave, with Eleanor's blessing, after realizing that if I didn't make a conscious break, I might be there for the rest of my life. That would mean I would always miss spring trout fishing because of preparations for our June dance recital.

Making a living in the sport-fishing field was next to impossible in those days, but sportsmen's show exhibitions were available to me and the Ashaway Line & Twine Company hired me to do part-time goodwill work, calling on their dealers. In 1954 I did a series of shows in the Midwest with Monte Blue, star of the silent screen, as emcee. When I showed up in my shorts, hip boots, and creel, which was everyone's idea of a girl fisherman's costume, Monte took me aside and told me he wanted to try something different. "Wear a dress," he said, "a long one, and we'll wow 'em." Leaping at the chance to portray casting as feminine, I bought a strapless, ankle-length white dress with silver leaves on it, high-heeled sandals, and, to complete the outfit, rhinestones for my hair.

The combination was perfect and Monte presented my act beautifully, speaking softly while I was casting of grace, timing, and beauty. I didn't cast at targets but, instead, used one rod and then two, creating as many interesting patterns with the fly lines as I could in time with music. *Up a Lazy River* was a natural, and the audiences responded. It couldn't last forever, though, and without either Monte or an orchestra the costume didn't play as well mixed in with lumberjacks, retrievers, and Sparky the seal. I changed back to the shorts, boots, and creel outfit—but I'll remember the gown and music as being the perfect way to depict fly casting as an art form, especially suitable for women.

So there I was, a young woman in a man's field, gaining notoriety because of it, and feeling I was where I wanted to be. I had lots to learn; my fishing experi-

ence was broad but shallow. My generation of young women did not venture alone into the woods or streams. There were also the difficulties of the costume for stream fishing, and the discomforts of biting insects and bad weather. The gear, in a man's size small, was uncomfortable and "bug dope," as it was called, was greasy and strong smelling. Because I loved being outdoors, I thought of it as paying the price to get the rewards, but I did not fish as often or as comfortably as a young man my age might have done. There have been remarkable advances in the area of comfort, for both men and women, in the last fifteen years.

In 1959, married and with one child, I took a part-time job with the Garcia Corporation, which was, then, the largest tackle company in the world. I lived in Florida at the time but my job was to promote their products, through clinics and exhibitions, anywhere in the country. Part of the job was to fish in tournaments and that was a real bonus. Just like any other woman, juggling a career and a family left me little time for recreational fishing.

Years later, as part of my work, I had the opportunity to appear in a film on giant bluefin-tuna fishing that Lee Wulff was producing for *ABC's American Sportsman* television series. Although Lee and I knew each other casually, it was our first opportunity to fish together. After our marriage in 1967, my fishing horizons expanded. We traveled to the West for trout, the Canadian Maritime Provinces and Iceland for Atlantic salmon, and to Ecuador for marlin. We became a team for Garcia and held fly-fishing clinics and programs for clubs throughout the country.

My presence attracted women to these events. In earlier generations, men had gone on fishing trips partly to "get away from the wife," but now fishermen asked me to direct my words to their wives or girlfriends, hoping to convert them into companions who could share the pleasure of fly fishing. In 1979 Lee and I opened a fly-fishing school in New York's Catskill Mountains. Soon one-quarter of our students were women, and that percentage has now risen to one-third.

It is estimated that there are two million committed fly fishermen in the United States. Only 10 per-

*In the quest for the perfect fishing hole, beautiful scenery is usually an afterthought. But sometimes an angler is lucky enough to find both, as this fisherman did by a waterfall in the Columbia River basin of Washington. (Photograph © Mark Kayser)*

cent of those, two hundred thousand or less, subscribe to the fly-fishing magazines, and readership is reported as 96 percent male. If as many as 50 or 60 percent of those male readers shares life with a woman, there is a great potential to swell our ranks. The greater the number of fly fisherwomen, the more likely it is that the manufacturers of equipment and clothing will cater to our special needs.

It has taken all of my life for the changes to develop in equipment and attitude that now make fly fishing a natural extension of a woman's love of the outdoors. Whether you are married to a fisherman or are a single woman, there is nothing to stop you now except lack of time. Fortunately, one of the strengths of our sex is our high tolerance for interruption....

Recently, artist Phyllis Sheffield, a friend who shares my love of dancing but who fishes only casually, listened patiently while I bubbled on about a recent fishing trip. "Joanie," she asked, "don't you *ever* get tired of fishing?" "No," I replied, "because it is always renewing!"

Sure, I can have enough of fishing on a tough day or in circumstances that are particularly uncomfortable, but I will never tire of what fishing gives me. It puts me in touch with another of nature's species, in beautiful surroundings that are as old as time. That is where I want to be; that is how I am renewed!

FACING PAGE: *With the sun on the rise, a fly fisherman casts into Washington's Lake Lenore. (Photograph © Dennis Frates)*

*Like father, like daughter: two anglers share a quiet moment discussing fly tying before wading into the river together. (Photograph © Larry Mishkar/Picture Smith)*

# NOT FAR
# FROM SUNDOWN

## By Arthur Gordon

Arthur Gordon has Georgia bred in his bones. A true Sourthern gentleman, he is a fifth-generation Georgia native and still lives in his hometown, the beautiful and historic city of Savannah.

Gordon has long worked as a magazine journalist, serving on the editorial staffs at *Cosmopolitan*, *Good Housekeeping*, and *Guideposts*, as well as a staff writer for *Reader's Digest*. Even boasting this venerable journalism background, writing about his great passion, the outdoors, remains almost a hobby.

From Savannah, Gordon can practically cast his line into the Atlantic Ocean, a proximity to the sea that has long nurtured his great love for saltwater surf fishing. "The fishing isn't what it used to be, but then, what is?" he notes.

This touching story originally appeared in *Field & Stream*.

*Casting into the surf, an angler is silhouetted against the brilliant glare of the ocean. (Photograph © Victor H. Colvard / The Green Agency)*

The old man came out of the Medical Arts building and walked slowly down to his car where the small black dog waited, paws on windowsill, ragged ears up, brown eyes following every movement. A welcoming tail thumped the upholstery.

"Move over, Andy," the old man said. He sat for a while gripping the wheel with hands that were thin but still strong. He looked up at the fierce sunlight gilding the weathervane on the courthouse down the street. "Ever had a cardiogram, Andy? Well, don't."

He had had others, of course, but this was the first since the blackouts had started, annoying little lapses, very quick, where darkness seemed to come at him from the outside corners of his eyes and everything faded but then gradually brightened again. He had said nothing to Martha—why alarm her?—but since she was away for a few days visiting the grandchildren he had decided to let the doctor check it out.

Now he almost wished he hadn't because the verdict was discouraging. No undue stress or excitement. No exertion. Specifically no more solitary expeditions down the lonely windswept beaches. "I know it'll be tough," the doctor said, "for you to give up surf fishing and messing around with boats. But slow-down time comes to all of us. Besides, you've already caught most of the fish in the sea, haven't you?" One of those questions designed to make you feel better that just make you feel worse.

"I suppose the man is right, Andy," the old man said. "But it's pretty annoying when a bunch of electric wires can tell you what to do. Look at that weathervane. Southeast wind; high tide around noon. One more little excursion won't make much difference, probably; why don't we try it before Miss Martha gets back and tells us we can't?"

In the little tidal river the skiff was 30 yards offshore. The old man flicked his surf-rod so that the 3-ounce sinker arched out and the leader wrapped itself around the anchor line close to the bow. He reeled in slowly until the keel of the skiff touched bottom, then looked at the dog sitting at the water's edge. "Come on, Andy," he said, "be brave. You may not be able to swim, but you can wade, can't you?"

Andy stood up, touched one paw to the water, then sat down again, looking dejected.

The old man sighed, picked Andy up, and deposited him in the boat. "Not only are you a coward," he said, "you are also the ugliest dog on the Eastern seaboard. Even your tail is hideous. How did I ever get stuck with a wretched beast like you?"

Andy looked up with soft brown eyes and wagged his hideous tail. He knew a compliment when he heard one.

The dog, just a stray which had been found half starving beside a road some years ago, went everywhere the old man went, even in the boat, although it was clear that some unknown early trauma had left him with a profound fear of water. Once the old man tried to overcome that fear by placing the dog on a tiny sandbar with a rising tide and the boat not 10 feet away. Years ago he had watched a mother raccoon teach her offspring to swim in such a manner, crossing a creek herself and then calling back to them until they found the courage to follow. But the misery in Andy's brown eyes as the water rose was more than he could stand, and in the end he placed the dog back in the skiff, where he sat immovably like a misplaced black fireplug until they were home and the old man carried him safely to shore.

Now he sat in just such fashion as the skiff drove through the chop in the middle of the river and then on through the network of creeks on the far side where terrapin skittered down the muddy banks into the still green water and mullet swirled and the great blue herons soared up and away. Ordinarily the old man paid little attention to such familiar things, but on this day he watched them with a certain intensity, as if trying to impress the images on his memory.

They came at last to a broad estuary flowing eastward through the barrier beaches with leaping tongues of surf on either side where it met the sea. A short distance above this entrance was a little cove, and here the old man anchored the boat, placing Andy carefully ashore and watching him chase sandpipers, barking wildly. He never yet had caught one, and never would, but the old man understood how he felt. A dream is just a belief in possibilities and this was Andy's dream.

He circled back at last to bark even more fiercely at a horseshoe crab, stranded on its back in a shallow pool. Seeing this, the old man paused. "Don't be rude to that crab, Andy," he said. "His ancestors were on this earth long before yours or mine. Besides, if we speak

*Fishermen try their luck in the saltwater shoreline shallows in this watercolor of fishing in the Florida Keys by painter Millard Wells.*

*A determined fisherman wades into the shoreline flats as the sun goes down. (Photograph © Dale C. Spartas/The Green Agency)*

*Walking the shore of "his" beach, Grandpa teaches the tricks of the trade to his granddaughter. (Photograph © Doug Stamm/ ProPhoto)*

nicely to him and help him out, the sea-gods may reward us." He picked up the grotesque creature by its armored tail, feeling the life vibrating within it still and carried it back toward the estuary with the dog pacing uneasily alongside. "Your mistake, Andy," he said, "is treating this crab as if it were an it, instead of thinking of it as a you. Try to get the notion through that head of yours that every living creature is a you, just as you are. Took me a long time to figure that out, but it sort of binds things together somehow. So let's just say, 'Good luck to you, old crab,'" and he tossed it out into deep water while Andy stared, bemused.

On then through some shallow dunes where the sea-oats nodded to their own shadows and across the broad beach, blinding white in the sun with scattered driftwood and bundles of marsh grass and bleached sanddollars. Two hundred yards offshore, gulls were mewing and diving where a school of mackerel were tearing up some baitfish. No other human being was in sight, no houses, no manmade thing except far off against the dunes the rusted engine of a wrecked shrimp boat. The old man knew that very few beaches like this could be found anywhere, and that this one could not remain untouched for very long, but he tried not to think about it.

Near the water's edge he put his gear on the sand and sat down beside it, waiting for his heart to cease its pounding. Ahead of him was a shallow lagoon or slough with the tide easing into it and beyond that a narrow sandbar where the green rollers broke with a sound like muffled thunder.

Andy came up, panting, and the old man poured some water from a small thermos and gave him a drink. "Nice day, isn't it, Andy? Nice friendly day. Nobody's trying to run us off today. But that was a queer business last year, wasn't it? Scared you, I know, and it spooked me too. Yessir, it did."

They had been fishing in this place on a bright autumn afternoon, wind and tide favorable, water so clear you could see schools of mullet stacked up in each wave as it curled over to break. The old man had made a few casts, at peace with himself, at peace with everything, waiting to see what the sea had to offer. Andy was sitting, tired of chasing sandpipers, content to wait as long as necessary.

Then without warning the sun seemed to grow dim. The green water turned the color of lead. The wind died, but the air seemed colder. The birds vanished. A ringing silence settled over everything. Waist deep in the warm water the old man felt the hair on the back of his neck tighten. He looked quickly, left and right, for a shark's fin, and then behind him. Nothing. But the feeling of isolation and dread grew stronger. On the beach Andy had crouched down suddenly like a dog expecting an undeserved blow. *This is nonsense*, the old man thought, but a deeper part of him knew that it was not. Something invisible was surrounding him, crowding in, something very powerful and very threatening. That something was laying claim to the special solitude of this place, and it didn't want to share it with any human being. Or any dog, either.

The old man had tried to close his mind against a rising tide of panic. He started backing up, reeling in, but suddenly the line was slack. He felt no strike, no tug, nothing, but he knew the hook and leader and sinker, were gone. He turned then and splashed back to the beach where Andy was still crouched beside the tackle box. He scooped up his gear and started back to the skiff, the dog close at his heels, angry with himself for fleeing but with a sense of almost-terror that was stronger than his anger. He put the dog in the boat, snatched up the anchor, cranked the engine, opened the throttle wide and roared westward up the estuary. And he did not look back.

His pulse seemed to be running smoothly and evenly now so he reached for his tackle box and took out a pair of pliers. "If this is the last roundup, Andy, why don't we even the odds a little bit?" Picking up the hook at the end of the long leader he carefully mashed the barb flat. "May cost us a fish or two, but that's all right." He took a piece of cut mullet and inserted the now barbless hook so that the needle point went through the skin at one place and came out at another. He stood up a bit stiffly. "If you had an ounce of fidelity in you," he said to Andy, "you'd swim this lagoon and join me on the bar. But I know you won't. Why couldn't I have had a noble retriever named Rex instead of a misbegotten mutt?" Andy lay down and put his nose on his forepaws. He judged words by tone, not content, and knew that all was well.

The old man waded across the lagoon, climbed the short steep bank on the far side, and moved into

*Some enchanted evening: A golden sunset and a glowing lantern are all the illumination this couple needs to do a bit of early-evening shore fishing together. (Photograph © Ron Spomer)*

the surf until the breakers swirled about his knees. The silver scales of the mullet glittered as the line soared out into deeper water. In a short time, now, the bar would be covered and the lagoon would be 5 feet deep. But the old man knew he had an hour of fishing before that, perhaps a bit more.

For 10 minutes he waited, feet braced against the thrust of the waves, cap brim pulled down over his eyes to lessen the sun-dazzle. A flight of pelicans came by, coasting downwind. Beyond the breakers the gleaming black backs of two porpoises surfaced and disappeared. The wind blew and the foam seethed softly and the tide moved in.

Abruptly, with a tremendous shock, something seized the bait. The rod bent almost double, then sprang erect again as a black-tipped shark, close to 5 feet, exploded into the air in a frenzy of spray, threw the hook, and was gone.

The old man felt his heart lurch with the sudden rush of adrenaline. He waited until it seemed quiet, then reeled in slowly. As he rebaited the hook, he noticed that his hands were trembling, so he waited until they were still before making another cast. Then he moved back six paces and waited again, because some instinct in him knew that the shark was only a prelude.

He knew this with certainty, and so he was not surprised when something picked up the bait gently and stealthily and started moving out to sea. He had disengaged the brake on the reel and was controlling the line only with his thumb, so he was able to apply pressure very gradually. But the pressure made no difference; the line kept moving out until he knew he would have to begin to fight the fish before it was all gone. So he flipped on the brake and struck hard.

It was like setting the hook into a runaway freight train. The reel gave a metallic screech; the line was ripped off despite the drag. The old man felt the tremendous pressure on his arms and shoulders and he knew that pressure must be maintained if he was going to land the fish. By aiding the drag with his thumb—and getting it burned—he managed to slow the first tremendous straightaway rush, but he knew that somehow he would have to turn the fish eventually. If it began to swim laterally, he might be able to move with it and eventually begin to recover some line. As it was he could see the linen backing through the few turns of monofilament that were left on the reel, and so he began to walk forward, following the fish. The water rose to his shoulders, a wave lashed him across the face and knocked his cap off. He still held the rod high and the strain was becoming unbearable when, far out, he saw the long dark shadow of his adversary silhouetted inside a towering roller, saw too the angry flash of a great bronze tail that could belong only to an enormous channel bass—stag bass, redfish, a fighter by any name.

The old man decided that he would either turn the fish or break the line. He put most of his remaining strength into a desperate heave, and the head of the fish swung round and it began to swim parallel to the beach, moving toward the point where the mouth of the lagoon met the incoming tide. The old man knew that he would never be able to land such a fish in the heavy surf. His only chance was to maneuver it into the lagoon itself. And after 20 minutes that is what he did, backing up slowly, hearing his own breath come in gasps, gaining 10 feet of line and losing 20, always keeping the tension on the fish until finally he could see it in the calm waters of the lagoon, where it made two or three last convulsive runs and then rolled over on its side, fins and tail moving faintly.

The old man waded forward slowly, feeling his knees tremble, keeping the rod tip high and the line taut. He came to the great fish and knelt beside it, knowing the mixture of triumph and regret that comes at such a time. He saw that the hook was embedded in a corner of the wide mouth, not far down the throat as he had feared. He said in a murmur, "You're pretty tired, aren't you, old fish? Believe me, so am I." He reached forward and removed the hook, but the exhausted bass made no lunge for freedom. It lay there, its yellow eye regarding its captor remotely.

"You'd like deeper water, wouldn't you?" the old man said finally. He put his rod down on the bottom of the lagoon—something he hated to do—and slid his arms under the passive fish. He eased its great weight gently out to a point where the water was 4 feet deep. He cradled it in his arms just under the surface where the sunlight glinted on the gill-plates, opening and closing, and the mother-of-pearl flanks and the massive tail with its two black spots. He waited, and gradually the fish righted itself as its strength came back. Finally it pulled away and began to swim, slowly at first, then faster and faster, toward the mouth of the lagoon and the open sea.

The old man stood up and watched it go. He turned, intending to look for the rod he had left underwater, but suddenly he felt dizzy and knew he had better get back to the bar while he could. He was within 3 feet of it when the darkness swept over him and he fell face down on the dry sand with his legs and feet still in the waters of the lagoon.

How long he lay there he did not know. Finally a shallow wave swirling across the bar slapped him in the face and he raised his head, choking and gasping. The darkness receded then and he came up on one elbow, glancing back toward the beach where his tackle box and spare rod rested tranquilly above the high-water mark. There was no sign of Andy, but when the old man sat up and scanned the now choppy waters of the lagoon, he saw a small black head moving toward him, ears flattened, eyes showing white with fright, submerged altogether now and then, but still coming, still swimming, closer and closer until the old man was able to reach forward and draw the shivering little animal into his lap. "Well done, Andy," he said. "I don't know how you thought you could help me, but I thank you for trying."

They sat there quietly for a little while. With his coat slicked back and his brown eyes, Andy looked almost like a baby seal. The old man could feel the dog's heart hammering furiously through his ribs. "Well, come on now," he said. "Better go back before it gets any deeper. Don't be afraid. I've got you and you've got me. We'll make it all right."

And so they did, the old man moving slowly through the current with one arm around Andy and one hand cupped under his chin, holding his head up until they came safely to the beach and made their way back to the skiff and home together. The old man wondered if from now on Andy might be a swimmer, but when they came to their final anchorage and he invited his companion to jump over and wade ashore, the invitation was declined. "Never mind, Andy," the old man said, carrying him to dry land. "We've had a good day. A very special kind of day."

That evening when he called Martha as he did every night when they were separated, the old man said nothing of what the day had held. It would keep until she got home. In fact, he thought, as he climbed wearily into bed and switched off the light, he might not tell anyone. Somehow it all might stay more intact if he didn't. He would know and Andy would know and that would be enough.

Andy was tired too. He went over to his scrap of carpet in the corner and lay down with a boneless thump. The old man smiled as he heard him sigh. He closed his eyes, then, and at once against the blackness inside his eyelids the great bronze fish swam through green and gold depths, striped now by shadow, tail and fins moving silently, remote and untroubled in the element where it belonged. Farther and farther away it moved, growing smaller and smaller until with a final mother-of-pearl flicker it was gone, and sleep came down like a benediction, and the long day was over.

# ANGLER SURVIVES IN A VEGETATIVE STATE

### By Henry Miller

Henry Edward Miller II is the outdoors writer for the Salem, Oregon, *Statesman Journal*, a post that handily mixes his hobbies of hunting and fishing with his craft of writing. Like Patrick F. McManus, Miller has a slightly sardonic eye with regards to goings-on in the great outdoors. As he philosophizes, "Fishing could best be described as a jerk on one end of a pole waiting for a jerk on the other end."

In 1998, Miller published a collection of his best newspaper columns entitled *Out of My Head (The neglected works of Henry Miller)*. The book's title plays on Miller's name, which he shares with the other, admittedly more famous—or infamous—Henry Miller, author of *Tropic of Cancer, The Air-Conditioned Nightmare*, and *The Rosy Crucifixion* trilogy.

This humorous column should be read as a warning. In this modern-day fable, Miller describes the effects being married to a rabid vegetarian may have on the unwary angler that lets his or her guard down.

*An angler fishes in a contemplative state from his dock. (Photograph © Richard Hamilton Smith)*

"Anybody home?" I asked, rapping on the door.

I was visiting my good friend and a former fishing fanatic, Milt Axelroot.

His wife, Sunflower Moonglow Kowalski-Axelroot, after an epic battle that lasted years, had converted Milt to vegetarianism a couple of months before. I thought I'd stop by and see how it was going.

Coming from the back yard was a swishing sound followed by the rending and tearing of plant life, much like the noises you hear on a National Geographic special when a herd of stampeding elephants flattens a banana plantation.

Peering around the corner of the house, I saw Milt, clad in waders and fishing vest, standing in his daughter's wading pool and making false casts over the garden with his favorite 9-foot, light-action graphite fly rod.

"Hi, Milt, how's it going?" I asked cheerily.

"Shhhhh," he said angrily. "You'll spook the cukes."

He launched a greenish fly into a tangle of vines, mended the slack, then reared back on the rod.

An 11-inch cucumber, impaled on the No. 6 hook, tore loose from a vine and wobbled and rolled across the lawn as Milt reeled in.

He scooped it up in a small trout landing net, detached the hook, admired it for a moment, then placed it gently into a wicker creel at his waist.

"A couple more like that and we'll have a dandy salad," Milt said with a grin.

"I took a 4-pound casaba from the same spot a couple of weeks ago," he said, gesturing toward a dirt mound of melon vines. "It was tricky getting it in, though. It wrapped the line around a sprinkler head while I was fighting it."

"I see you've made the adjustment to being a nature nutloaf," I observed as Milt began false-casting again, shifting his position in the wading pool.

"Yea. It was tough. When Sunflower told me I'd have to give up fishing and hunting, the marriage almost went into the dumper.

"But with little Lotus Ankh just turning 4, and the community-property laws being what they are, this seemed like a more acceptable compromise."

It wasn't easy at first, Milt said, allowing the line to shoot out into the garden.

He said he had to set up his fly bench to tie tomato horn worm and apple maggot imitations.

*A fisherman casts his line into the waters of Polly Lake in Minnesota's Boundary Waters Canoe Area. (Photograph © Richard Hamilton Smith)*

*Surrounded by pine-covered mountains, a fisherman trolls the tranquil waters of Salmon Bay Lake in the Tongass National Forest on Alaska's Prince of Wales Island. (Photograph © Roy Corral)*

And it was during one outing to test the apple flies that the police arrested him casting over an abandoned Grannie Smith orchard near Corvallis, Milt said.

His explanation to the officers led to a 72-hour hold for psychiatric observation at the Oregon Home for the Bewildered, he continued. But once Sunflower showed up and explained what was going on, the justice system relented.

Since then, things have been going along pretty smoothly, Milt said.

"I caught a mess of tomatoes with a couple of cabbage butterfly imitations this morning," he said. "A couple of them were pretty small, but I had to keep them because they were pulp-hooked."

Milt said he was pretty busy most nights tying up his assortment of agricultural pest imitations for his upcoming vacation.

The family was planning a tour of U-pick farms in northeastern Oregon and southern Washington, he explained.

"Missing real fishing isn't so bad," Milt said, a shade of wistfulness in his voice. "Hell, next week I'm going out on a charter boat out of Depoe Bay to go kelp fishing.

"And a healthy-sized kohlrabi or carrot will give you a good fight trying to get it out of the ground, especially on light tackle."

Milt began false-casting again over a likely looking stand of pole beans, which he referred to as the panfish of the vegetable kingdom.

"It takes a mess of them to make a meal," he said, detaching a wax bean from the hook and adding it to the creel.

I decided to leave him to his fun, but I couldn't resist asking just one more question.

"Milt, I can see you've adjusted pretty well to being a compost head when it comes to fishing," I said. "But you were such a hunting fanatic. How did you learn to live without that?"

A grin spread on his face from ear-to-ear.

"Come on inside the house," he said, reeling up the line and tucking the fly rod under his arm. "I'll show you my 14-pound watermelon. I had the rind mounted.

"I got it right through the stem at 150 yards. Didn't ruin any of the meat."

# A SPECIAL MUSKIE!

### By Bob Becker

Bob Becker writes in the foreword to his evocative collection *Fishing Stories: Adventures on Lakes and Streams* (1994) that "I didn't learn to love fishing. I was born loving fishing." Those two sentences serve as a fitting introduction to Becker and his essays.

Becker served for more than three decades with the Wisconsin Department of Natural Resources. After his retirement, he began a second career as a writer and has published two compilations of nostalgic lore, *Grandpa's Stories* (1991) and *Ya, Ya! Those Were the Days* (1993).

Living in Wisconsin, Becker has had ample opportunity to sample both lakes and streams—as well as the odd foray to troll the reefs of the Bahamas and cast into the surf of the North Carolina coast. In the end, however, nothing haunts him as much as the muskellunge, one special catch being the subject of this essay.

*A muskellunge (a.k.a. muskie) attacks a lure with characteristic ferocity. Muskies are close relations to the northern pike but are less abundant. Their rarity, combined with their large size and renowned fighting ability, make them a coveted catch. (Photograph © Doug Stamm/ProPhoto)*

The muskie mount came home the other day. Jack Thompson did a good job on it. It's back is arched, and it's toothy mouth is open just as it was a second before it struck my bait that sunny afternoon last September on Sand Lake.

Now, I'm not a trophy fisherman. Over the past 50 years I've caught my share of fish, but this is the first one I've put on the wall. And that may not have happened either had not Momma talked me into it by saying she'd give it to me for Christmas.

It's not a real bragging fish—only 19 pounds and just under 42 inches. But it was a beautifully formed and marked fish. And besides, it was a special fish.

I was fishing with Art "Mr. Muskie" Oehmcke that day. Art spent a lifetime propagating muskies, and it's because of efforts such as his that we know muskie fishing as the quality sport that it is today.

Fall was just coming into its glory that September day. The color was coming on, and the red and gold hues along the shore gave the lake a full-screen technicolor look. A gentle breeze ruffled the water's surface, and a wool shirt felt good.

Sand is one of "my" lakes. I've put a lot of hours on it, and I know it well. How many memories of fish raised here and fish caught there! Art had never fished it; and so it was that we found ourselves drifting over its bars and weedbeds.

Talk went back and forth from old times to new times as we methodically heaved the big baits, retrieved them, always watching for that "follow." Experienced muskie fishermen are realists. They know how many sore arms and backaches go into putting a keeper in the boat. We fished steadily but casually, pausing only to change baits when water conditions warranted a deeper or shallower running lure.

Than, as always, out of nowhere it happened. I was casting a muskie-size Rapala, one of my favorite baits. In the clear water I saw the fish rush the bait and strike.

Instinctively I leaned into the heavy rod to set the hook—perhaps a little too instinctively! Because as the fish passed under the boat, all I could see was 3½ feet of muskie with a foot of Rapala sticking out of its mouth.

"I'll never get 'em, Art!" I said. "He's not hooked good!"

"Take him slow!" came the counsel of Mr. Muskie. He'd been there before.

*This Minnesota lake may seem calm and serene, but beneath its serene ripples lives a large, ornery monster ready to strike. These anglers could suddenly find their peaceful morning interrupted by a muskie seizing their walleye or bass catch. (Photograph © Richard Hamilton Smith)*

So with a feather touch on the reel, I played the fish. No pressure, no horsing. Ever so slowly, I nursed the fish up and toward the boat.

Art stood ready with the big, long-handled net; and when the fish swirled on the surface the first time; the net shot out, and the fish came twisting and turning into the boat. I didn't think a 70 year-old duffer could move that fast!

There were the usual "All rights!", the hand shake, and the admirations of what a pretty fish it was. And I remember remarking about the large stomach bulge, wondering what was in it.

That was the action for the day. That night the fish was hung on the scale at the SuperValu in Spooner and the pictures taken of two tired but smiling fishermen. And that's when Momma told me to have it mounted.

So the call went out to Jack Thompson who has his taxidermy shop out east of Spooner, and a couple days later I brought the frozen fish out to him.

A few days later I stopped in again to pick up the meat from the fish.

"What was in that fish?" I asked.

"You'd never believe this," he said. "That fish had a full-grown female bufflehead duck in its stomach!"

Like I said, it was a special muskie. How often do you catch a fish and a duck on the same cast?

*With its tigerlike strips glowing even underwater, a muskie lurks in its lair, waiting for the next unsuspecting carp, yellow perch, bullhead—or duck—to cross its path. (Photograph © Doug Stamm/ProPhoto)*

Below: *Two young anglers work to keep their hole free of ice and lure in their catch while ice fishing on Minnesota's Lake Winnebago. (Photograph © Richard Hamilton Smith)*

## The Glory and Misery of Ice Fishing

There has been little written on the fine art of ice fishing. It is not a style of fishing that lends itself to poetry or beautiful prose. Still, if you inhabit the northern climes where winter ice freezes over a perfectly good lake for several months of the year, you might as well as get out your auger, drop a line, and join the fun.

*Two fisherman cut holes through the ice of Washington's Cascade Reservoir. (Photograph © William H. Mullins)*

Above: *Ice fishing requires true dedication. The ice fisherman and -woman must brave the elements to while away the hours in the seclusion of this winter home away from home. Here is a collection of ice-fishing equipment you might have found in an ice-fishing house in the 1930s, including a handmade wooden rod, two steel rods and reels made by Stubby, scoops, auger, sled, snowshoes, a 1933 copy of* National Sportsman *magazine, and a 1920s model Coleman lantern with hand pump. The heated minnow bucket was an especially creative invention; inside the insulated metal bucket was a miniature kerosene lantern that kept the water from freezing and the minnows fresh for deep-winter fishing. Memorabilia owner: Pete Press. (Photograph © Howard Lambert)*

*Spear fishing is usually done in the cold of winter on the thin ice of shallow bays, channels, and inlets. The decoys are used to draw in fish, which are then skewered by a spear such as the handmade one pictured. These decoys are used to lure sturgeon into the range of the spearhandler. (Photograph © Richard Hamilton Smith)*

# MY FIRST-TIME
# FLYFISHING DISASTER

By P. J. O'Rourke

P.J. O'Rourke is a fly fisherman—and he has the receipts to prove it.

One of America's premier humorists, O'Rourke is a reactionary, an idealist, a Republican, and a downright funny guy. He was the editor of the *National Lampoon* and the foreign affairs desk chief of *Rolling Stone*. Along the way he has published a small library of books of political commentary, journalism, and humor, including such essential reading as *Parliament of Whores: A Lone Humorist Attempts to Explain the Entire U.S. Government* (1991), *All the Trouble in the World: The Lighter Side of Overpopulation, Famine, Ecological Disaster, Ethnic Hatred, Plague, and Poverty* (1994), *Age and Guile Beat Youth, Innocence, and a Bad Haircut* (1995), *The Bachelor Home Companion: A Practical Guide to Keeping House Like a Pig* (1997), and *Eat the Rich* (1998), among others.

This essay on his trials and tribulations—mostly tribulations—as a budding fly fisherman first appeared in *Sports Afield* and proves that he is still budding.

*The signs of a veteran angler: perfect reel, classic bamboo rod, and a wicker creel. (Photograph © William H. Mullins)*

I'D NEVER FLYFISHED. I'd done other kinds of fishing. I'd fished for bass. That's where I'd get far enough away from the dock so that people couldn't see there wasn't any line on my pole, then drink myself blind in the rowboat. And I'd deep-sea fished. That's where the captain would get me blind before we'd left the dock, and I'd be the one who couldn't see the line. But I'd never flyfished.

I'd always been of two minds about the sport. On the one hand, here's a guy standing in cold water up to his liver, throwing the world's most expensive string at trees. A full two-thirds of his time is spent untangling stuff, which he could be doing in the comfort of his own home with old shoelaces. The whole business costs like sin and requires heavier clothing. Furthermore, it's conducted in the middle of blackfly season. Cast and swat. Cast and swat. Flyfishing may be a sport invented by insects with flyfishermen as bait. And what does the truly sophisticated dry-fly artist do when he finally bags a fish? He lets it go and eats baloney sandwiches instead.

On the other hand, flyfishing did have its attractions. I love to waste time and money. I had ways to do this most of the year—hunting, skiing, renting summer houses in To-Hell-and-Gone Harbor for a Lebanon hostage's ransom. But, come spring, I was limited to cleaning up the yard. Even with a new Toro every two years and a lot of naps by the compost heap, it's hard to waste much time and money doing this. And then there's the gear needed for flyfishing. I'm a sucker for anything that requires more equipment than I have sense. My workshop is furnished with the full panoply of power tools, all bought for the building of one closet shelf in 1979.

When I began to think about flyfishing, I realized I'd never be content again until my den was cluttered with computerized robot flytying vises, space-age Teflon and ceramic knotless tapered leaders, sterling-silver English fish scissors and 35 volumes on the home life of the midge. And there was one other thing. I'm a normal male who takes an occasional nip; therefore, I love to put funny things on my head. Sometimes it's the nut dish, sometimes the spaghetti colander, but the hats I'd seen flyfishermen wear were funnier than either, and I had to have one.

I went to Hackles & Tackle, an upscale dry-fly specialty shop that also sells fish-print wallpaper and cashmere V-necked sweaters with little trout on them. I got a graphite rod for about the price of a used car and a reel made out of the kind of exotic alloys that you can go to jail for selling to the wrong people. I also got one of those fishing vests that come down only to the top of your beer gut and look like you dressed in the dark and tried to put on your 10-year-old son's three-piece suit. And I purchased lots of monofilament and teensy hooks covered in auk down and moose lint, and an entire L. L. Bean boat bag full of flyfishing do-whats. I also brought home a set of flyfishing how-to videotapes. What better way to take up a sport than from a comfortable armchair? That's where I'm at my best with most sports anyway.

There were three tapes. The first one claimed it would teach me to cast. The second would teach me to "advanced-cast." And the third would tell me where trout live, how they spend their weekends and what they'd order for lunch if there were underwater delicatessens for fish. I started the VCR, and a squeaky little guy with an earnest manner and a double-funny hat came on, heaving flyline around, telling me the secret to making beautiful casting loops is . . .

Whoever made these tapes apparently assumed I knew how to tie backing to reel and line to backing and leader to line and so on, all the way out to the little feather and fuzz that fish sometimes eat at the end. I didn't even know how to put my rod together. I had to go to the children's section at the public library and check out My *Big Book of Fishing* and begin with how to open the package it all came in.

A triple granny got things started on the spool. After 12 hours and help from pop rivets and a tube of Krazy Glue, I managed an Albright knot between backing and line. But my version of a nail knot in the leader put Mr. Gordian, of ancient-Greek-knot-legend fame, strictly on the shelf. It was the size of a hamster and resembled one of the Woolly Bugger flies I'd bought, except it was in the size you use for killer whales. I don't want to talk about blood knots and tippets. There I was with two pieces of invisible plastic, trying to use fingers the size of jumbo hot dogs while holding a magnifying glass and a Tensor lamp between my teeth and gripping nasty tangles of monofilament with each big toe. My girlfriend had to come over and cut me

*Readying their gear by the warmth of the stove, two Alaskan fly fishermen prepare for another day's work. (Photograph © Ron Spomer)*

out with pinking shears. I've decided I'm going to get one of those nine-year-old Persian kids they use to make incredibly tiny knots in fine Bokhara rugs and just take her with me on all my fishing trips.

I rewound Mr. Squeaky and started over. I was supposed to keep my rod tip level and keep my rod swinging in a 90-degree arc. When I snapped my wrist forward, I was giving a quick flick of a blackjack to the skull of a mugging victim. When I snapped my wrist back, I was sticking my thumb over my shoulder and telling my brother-in-law to get the hell out of here, and I mean right now, buster. Though it wasn't explained with so much poetry.

Then I was told to try a "yarn rod." This was some-

thing else I'd bought at the tackleshop. It looked like a regular rod tip from a two-piece rod but had a cork handle. You run a bunch of bright orange yarn through the guides and flip it around. It's supposed to imitate a flyrod in slow motion. I don't know about that, but I do know you can catch and play a nine-pound house cat on a yarn rod, and it's great sport. They're hard to land, however. And I understand cat fishing is strictly catch and release if they're under 20 inches.

After 60 minutes of videotape, seven minutes of yarn-rod practice, 25 minutes of cat fishing and several beers, I felt I was ready. I picked up the fin tickler and laid out a couple of loops that weren't half bad, if I do say so myself. I'll bet I cast almost three times before making macramé out of my weight-forward Cortland 444. This wasn't so hard.

I also watched the advanced tape. But Squeaky had gone grad school on me. He's throwing reach casts, curve casts, roll casts, steeple casts and casts he calls "squiggles" and "stutters." He's writing his name with the line in the air. He's pitching things forehand, backhand and between his wader legs. And, through the magic of video editing, every time his hook-tipped dust kitty hits the water, he lands a trout the size of a canoe.

The videotape about trout themselves wasn't much use either. It's hard to get excited about where trout feed when you know the only way you're going to be able to get a fly to that place is by throwing your flybox at it.

I must say, however, all the tapes were informative. "Nymphs and streamers" are not, as it turns out, naked mythological girls decorating the high-school gym with crepe paper. And I learned that the part of flyfishing I'm going to be best at is naming the flies: Blue Wing Earsnag; Overhanging Brush Muddler; Royal Toyota Hatchback; O'Rourke's Ouchtail; and PJ's Live Worm-'n'-Bobber.

By now I'd reached what they call a "learning plateau." If I was going to catch a fish, I had to either go get in the water or open the fridge and toss hooks at Mrs. Paul's frozen haddock fillets. I made reservations at a famous fishing lodge on the Au Sable River in Michigan. When I got there and found a place to park among the Saabs and Volvos, the proprietor said I was just a few days early for the Hendrickson hatch. There is, I've learned, one constant in all fishing, which is: The time the fish are biting is almost—but not quite—now.

I looked pretty good making false casts in the lodge parking lot. I mean, no one laughed out loud. But most of the other 2000 young professionals fishing this no-kill stretch of the Au Sable were pretty busy checking to make sure that their trout shirts were color-coordinated with their Reebok wading sneakers.

When I stepped into the river, however, my act came to pieces. My line hit the water like an Olympic belly-flop medalist. I hooked four "tree trout" in three minutes. My backcasts had people ducking for cover in Traverse City. The only thing I could manage to get a drag-free float on was me after I stepped into a hole. And the trout? The trout laughed.

The next day I could throw tight loops, sort of aim, even make a gentle presentation and get the line to lie right every so often. But when I tried to do all of these things at once, I looked like I was conducting "Flight of the Bumblebee" in fast-forward. I was driving tent pegs with my rod tip. My slack casts wrapped around my thighs. My straight-line casts went straight into the back of my neck. My improved surgeon's loops looked like full Windsors. I had wind knots in everything, including my Red Ball suspenders. And $200 worth of fly floatant, split-shot, Royal Coachmen and polarized sunglasses fell off my body and were swept downstream.

Then, *mirabile dictu,* I hooked a fish. I was casting some I-forget-the-name nymph and clumsily yanking it in when my rod tip bent and my pulse shot into trade-deficit numbers. I lifted the rod—the first thing I'd done right in two days—and the trout actually leaped out of the water as if it were trying for a *Fly Fisherman* playmate centerfold. I sounded like my little sister in the middle of a puppy litter: "Ooooo, that's a baby, yessssssss, come to Daddy, wooogie-woogie-woo." It was a rainbow, and I'll bet it was seven inches long. All right, five. Anyway, when I grabbed the thing, some of it stuck out of both sides of my hand. I hadn't been so happy since I passed my driver's-license exam.

So I'm a flyfisherman now. Of course, I'm not an expert yet. But I'm working on the most important part of flyfishing technique—boring the hell out of anybody who'll listen.

*"You will find angling to be like the virtue of humility, which has a calmness of spirit and a world of other blessings attending upon it." —Izaak Walton,* The Compleat Angler *(Photograph © Alan and Sandy Carey)*

ABOVE: *A fly fisherman pauses briefly to tie a new fly to his line. (Photograph © Bill Buckley/The Green Agency)*

LEFT: *The line of a fly fisherman dances above the water of Arizona's Colorado. (Photograph © Ron Spomer)*

# FALL FISHING

## By Lynette Dodson with Colleen Story

Lynette Dodson is the first to admit that she actually likes to fish with worms. Her co-author Colleen Story may be a devoted fly fisherwoman, but Dodson "grew up with worms," as she proudly states.

From this divergent starting point, the duo share many things in common. Dodson is a fourth-generation Montanan and Story's great-grandparents homesteaded in the Treasure State. Dodson is a freelance writer, filmmaker, and mother; her articles have appeared in the New York *Times Magazine* and *Montana* magazine. Story is a quiltmaker and mother.

Still, the fundamental dichotomy between anglers who place their bets on the lowly worm or the high-falutin' fly remains—and inspired this story. The tall tale is one in a series chronicling the adventures and misadventures of the two owners of the Your Big Butt Broke My Bed & Breakfast. This piece originally appeared in *Firestarter News and Review* from Livingston, Montana.

*Armed with their handy travel-sized fishing rods and reels, two anglers prepare for a day chasing the big catch. Photographer Wayne Gudmundson looks through his viewfinder with a wry eye in his numerous books, including this image from* Minnesota Gothic. *(Photograph © Wayne Gudmundson)*

Days had grown shorter, nights had grown longer. Grass which had once stood green and flush with moisture now lay flat and brown, scorched by months of intense mountain sun. Leaves crunched underfoot as schoolchildren tramped tardily to class. The essence of burning ranches wafted over the valley; summer's end, and fall's fishing, had come to the bustling riverside community.

On a sleepy residential side street, two khaki-clad manly figures were carefully unloading the yawning back side of their luxury recreation vehicle. Gortex, neoprene, nylon, polar fleece—a seemingly never-ending stream of high-end catalog purchases constructed from petroleum products flowed onto the street. This innocuous activity had aroused the curiosity of the inhabitants of the nosy neighborhood, while alarming the proprietors of Your Big Butt Broke My Bed & Breakfast.

"Range Rover?" questioned Linnie in a complaining tone.

"Golden Trout Mountain Lodge said they were sending their overflow right over," Kate explained.

"Overflow?" Linnie replied with disdain. "I'd say its more like backwash."

The bed and breakfast owners launched instantly into crow-like cackling, drawing the gentlemen's attention to their porch.

"After they get unloaded, we've gotta get them to move that thing into the alley," whispered Kate to her partner before hollering half-heatedly to their now sweating customers, "You guys need any help?"

One gentleman paused to comment before dabbing his brow with a silk bandanna. "If you want a tip."

"Jeez, doesn't anybody use motels anymore?" Linnie muttered under her breath as she and Kate leaped off the porch to assist their guests.

"You mean besides the locals?" quipped Kate as she gingerly stepped over a child's battered bicycle monopolizing the sidewalk.

The two small-business owners found themselves blinded by the glare of the gentlemen's highly pumiced complexions as the "yupsters" (as Kate and Linnie referred to this type of clientele) turned to greet their hostesses. The effect was further enhanced when the two men grimaced, revealing a full range of brilliant white teeth bespeaking years of meticulous dental care. Linnie made a quick mental note to reapply for Medicaid.

Perusing the mountain of monogrammed luggage, Kate quickly inquired, "So, which one of you guys is Eddie?"

"Eddie?" replied one of the new arrivals.

"Yeah, Eddie. Eddie Bauer."

"Cabela ..." interjected Linnie, "that's Spanish, isn't it?"

Stunned by the women's consumer naïveté, the fishing aficionados quickly recovered to make their own introductions.

"John Philip Whitebread IV."

"John Thoroughbred Mayonnaise V."

"I'm Linnie, and this is my partner Kate," said the blonde, pointing to her dark-haired companion.

"Partner?" quizzed John Whitebread. "Oh you two must be ..."

"Yes," interrupted Linnie, "we're in business together. We own Your Big Butt Broke My Bed & Breakfast."

"Where on earth did you ever come up with a name like that?" wondered John Mayonnaise.

"It's a long story," Kate replied. Tired of standing in the street, she made a grab for one of the smaller parcels and headed back into the house.

"The cabernet!" shrieked the Johns in unison.

"That's wine you've got there, Kate," restaurant veteran Linnie advised the disappearing figure.

"She'll disrupt the sediment," moaned Mayonnaise.

"Don't worry, I'll put it in the fridge," was the reply from the bowels of the bed and breakfast.

Horrified, the connoisseurs raced into the house and straight through a sophisticated construction of Legos and crayons. Catching a new, unnamed color under his yacht shoe, Whitebread found himself propelled into the kitchen area before everyone else.

"Boy, are the kids gonna be pissed," commented Linnie surveying the wreckage with dismay.

Kate launched a barrage of conversation. "They were so excited to have fishing guests they went right out into the garden and started digging for worms. Thank God we saved the sparrow that died last week—those maggots should be just about ripe ..."

Mayonnaise helped Whitebread up from the floor. "I think there's been a mistake," commented the more agile guest.

Kate—with the long overdue power bill check she

*Bobbers came in every shape, size, and color imaginable. While simple, they are also simply pleasing—they are prime examples of American folk art. Memorabilia owner: Pete Press. (Photograph © Howard Lambert)*

had already postdated and dropped in the mail in mind—made a quick recovery: "No way! You guys ain't going nowhere!"

Linnie, pondering the significance of Kate's double negative, grabbed a plain brown shopping bag from the kitchen table and began pulling out items. "Look, we've got peanut butter, marshmallows, Cheese Whiz . . ."

"Both regular and nacho-flavored too!" added Kate.

"Yeah, we went all out for you guys," Linnie hurriedly continued.

Snickering, John Mayonnaise replied, "You don't actually expect us to eat that stuff, do you?"

It was Kate and Linnie's turn to laugh. "Hell no! It's *bait*!"

This last word was the final straw for the yupsters. With a disgusted shake of his coiffed silver locks, Whitebread reached into his pleated bellows pocket and pulled out a cell phone. "What's the number for Golden Trout Lodge?"

The girls were crushed, but only momentarily so. At that instant a sickening metal brushing sound, like thousands of crazed rodents galloping on an unoiled treadmill, came from the direction of the street.

"What in heaven's name is that?" wondered one of the Johns.

Kate turned to Linnie and asked in a concerned tone, "What day is this?"

Before Linnie could reply, unearthly, bloodcurdling, high-tech screams were emitted from the street. Everyone raced outside in time to witness the final crunching of the fishermen's gear under the rear wheels of the city's street sweeper. To add insult to injury, the flapping tail end of the Range Rover was disappearing around the corner, hauled off by an unmarked tow truck.

While Linnie slipped back into the house to check her homeowner's insurance policy, Kate wisely suggested, "Let's go fishin'!"

Later, by a culvert at the nearby slough, the fishing gang had arranged themselves under shedding cottonwood trees, each sitting in a lawn chair that had only just recently been even further marked down at a local dis-count store. For several hours both Kate and Linnie had been fishing their guts out, casting lures and live (and frozen) bait into the slow-moving, murky waters. Meanwhile, John Mayonnaise alternately pouted and perspired profusely while John Whitebread had continuous phone conversations with various Washington, D. C. attorneys.

"Hey John M., hand me another Elk Hide from the cooler, will ya?" Linnie asked while adjusting her bobber.

Kate pulled the stringer out of the water and proudly displayed the day's catch. "Dinner's on us guys."

Mayonnaise shuddered while Whitebread shook his head. Covering the cell phone's receiver, he admitted, "Sorry ladies, we're into 'catch and release.'"

Nonapologetically, Kate replied, "We do 'keep and eat' around here."

Then, for a short time silence fell upon the mismatched couples. It was late afternoon. Sunlight filtered through the remaining foliage on the decades-old trees surrounding the slough. Magpies conversed on draping branches. No-see-ums flitted on exposed skin. Magic hour and the end of another six-pack was approaching. Glancing in the direction of the Easterners, Linnie thought back to an old saying from her high school days: "Everything looks better after a few Elk Hides." Feeling competitive, her hand wrapped around another cold one, the Montana native provokingly queried, "Hey Mayo, wanna chuggalug?"

His thirsty and competitive spirit aroused, Mayonnaise reached into the Styrofoam cooler. Pushing aside milk cartons full of night crawlers and ziploc bags stuffed with bullheads, he pulled out a can. Linnie and John M. both popped their tops and raced their cans to their mouths.

Kate remembered something important. "Hey, John W., can I use your phone?" In between calls, Whitebread reluctantly gave his cellular up and found a Zebco in his hand instead. After the initial repulse of holding a spinning reel in his hand, Whitebread was even more horrified to find the sensation becoming familiar. Not quite consciously aware of what he was doing, Whitebread took a nostalgic cast into the slough.

A flood of childhood memories bubbled forth.

*With a boulder in the center of a stream as a chair, an angler ties on a new fly. (Photograph © Jim Noelker/The Green Agency)*

*A warm autumn day has lured another angler to Colorado's Frying Pan River. (Photograph © Robert E. Barber)*

*The sun may be dipping below the horizon, but there is still time for one more cast. (Photograph © Bill Marchel)*

Remembrances of long summer days spent with family and friends on the banks of unnamed lakes and anonymous ponds, tossing a line—and all the cares in the world—into rippling waters, just kicking back to let it all happen; a bite, a strike, then reeling in another big one to hook on the stringer. John Whitebread remembered a time when he could catch his limit.

Meanwhile, John Mayonnaise was having difficulty finding his limit—of Elk Hides. He and Linnie were standing at the edge of the slough testing a set of X-ray vision fishing glasses. "Look, a sucker!" shouted Linnie, pointing under a clump of moss.

Kate, just off the phone with the kids, announced gleefully, "Wesson and Wyatt are bringing the Pocket Fisherman and some inner tubes down so we can do some deeper water fishing."

"That means some serious sinkers . . ." Whitebread commented sagely.

". . . and bigger bobbers," finished Mayonnaise.

Surprised, but pleasantly so, by the Johns' attitude adjustment, Kate commented, "All this bait talk is making me hungry."

Linnie glanced shyly towards Whitebread on her left, then to Mayonnaise on her right. "You guys wanna sandwich?"

Later on in the week, the girls were sitting around the kitchen table. Kate began listing the household accounts payable, which were finally going to be paid. "Let's see, there's the power bill, the phone bill, the garbage bill, the veterinary bill, and . . ." pausing for effect, "it looks like some of us get to visit the dentist."

Linnie stared wistfully out the window at one of the cats digging in the children's sandbox. "Gee, those guys weren't half bad, were they?"

Intuitively, Kate knew what her partner was thinking.

"Hope they make it back for the big cheese ball hatch next spring."

# WHY I FISH

By Ron Schara

Ron Schara's love for the outdoors is broadcast over numerous media. For almost three decades, he covered the outdoors beat for the Minneapolis *Star Tribune* newspaper. He then moved into television journalism, hosting the national cable magazine show *Minnesota Bound* on the Outdoor Life Network as well as the the number-one-rated *Call of the Wild* storytelling show for the Outdoor Channel and ESPN's *Backroads with Ron & Raven*.

Schara grew up in northeast Iowa's rugged bluff country and has earned degrees in journalism and fish and wildlife biology. Today, he contributes to the public forum on many environmental issues and is never shy to take a stand to preserve the outdoors. Schara also holds strong beliefs for introducing children to the hunting and fishing world, and hosts clinics for children sponsored by Gander Mountain, WalMart, and others.

Schara's heartfelt essay from "Minnesota Bound" provides an ideal conclusion to this anthology chronicling one hundred years of fishing.

*Sunrise at the "office": an angler works Oregon's Mann Lake. (Photograph © Dennis Frates)*

WHY DO I fish? It's a fair questions but it's not an easy answer.

For one thing, we anglers are seldom asked to explain what keeps us casting, keeps us hoping to catch something. It's no mystery to us. Perhaps the only people who are puzzled by fishing are those who don't do it.

It's been said the essence of fishing is much more than casting or retrieving or playing your catch. It's the wind in your face, they say, the sound of awakening birds as the sun peeks over the horizon. In every fishy place there is magic and mystery—just waiting to be discovered by the next angler to come along. But the quest to unlock those fishy secrets takes you to nifty places and easily some of the world's garden spots. And let's not forget the pure joy of catching, that moment when a fishing dream is dancing on the end of the line. Memories are made of this.

Fishing is also a teacher. The lessons learned in a fishing boat are not lost when you return to shore. For example, patience is a big lesson. Patience is absolutely required to be an angler. But you also learn that patience pays. Going fishing is also a lesson in humility. Put another way, to fish is to be humbled—not once but time and time again. But that's fine. Such lessons taught by fish help keep life itself in perspective.

Sure, some of us who fish are known to exaggerate a fish or two. An exact truth isn't really necessary to tell a good fish story. But remember this, for every exaggerated tale of giant whoppers caught and stuffed, there are the many true stories about the big one that got away.

Beyond the big fish and big fibs, there is also a spiritual and eternal side to this pursuit we call angling. Clearly, fishing is a pursuit of a lifetime. You're never too young to start. And you're never too old to quit. I like that about fishing. As my own fishing seasons wind down to a precious few, it's nice to know I'll be there, be there as long as I can. As long as I can bait a hook and make a cast, as long as I am living, I intend to be fishing.

*Undaunted by the chill winds of the Great Lakes, an angler fishes along a Lake Michigan pier. (Photograph © Richard Hamilton Smith)*

*A day down at the old fishing hole from a 1950s Massey-Harris tractor brochure.*

*A day down at the old fishing hole from a 1950s Massey-Harris tractor brochure.*

# PERMISSIONS

OVERLEAF: *A fisherman and his golden retriever reel in the last rainbow trout of the day. (Photograph © Alan and Sandy Carey)*